# COSMIC!

BUCKINGHAMSHIRE

Edited by Simon Harwin

First published in Great Britain in 1999 by
POETRY NOW YOUNG WRITERS
1-2 Wainman Road, Woodston,
Peterborough, PE2 7BU
Telephone (01733) 230748

All Rights Reserved

Copyright Contributors 1998

HB ISBN 0 75430 251 2
SB ISBN 0 75430 252 0

FOREWORD

With over 63,000 entries for this year's Cosmic competition, it has proved to be our most demanding editing year to date.

We were, however, helped immensely by the fantastic standard of entries we received, and, on behalf of the Young Writers team, thank you.

The Cosmic series is a tremendous reflection on the writing abilities of 8-11 year old children, and the teachers who have encouraged them must take a great deal of credit.

We hope that you enjoy reading *Cosmic Buckinghamshire* and that you are impressed with the variety of poems and style with which they are written, giving an insight into the minds of young children and what they think about the world today.

CONTENTS

Beechview Middle School
- Kabir Jahan — 1
- Adeyinka Ogunekun — 1
- Kylie Twitchen — 2
- Siobhan Miles — 2
- Katie Marmion — 3
- Charlotte Farmer — 3
- Sukhwinder K Banser — 4
- Rochelle Williams — 4
- Paul Galbraith — 5
- Sara Asady — 5
- Kerry Norwood — 6
- Gemma Giadom — 7
- Timmy Lavelle — 8
- Jasmine White — 8
- Neil Johnston — 9

Bierton CE Combined School
- James Hollings — 9
- Emma Ward — 10
- Hayley Morris — 10
- Adam Llewellyn — 11
- Kristian Purdie — 11
- Julia Padget — 12
- Thomas Simonds — 12
- Sarah Cosby — 13
- Nicola Evans — 14
- Christopher Crawford — 14
- Charlotte Handy — 15
- Annabel Vooght — 16
- Emma Piotrowski — 17
- Hannah Scrimshaw — 17
- Lorna Kelleher — 18
- Amanda Young — 18

Bourton Meadow Combined School

Richard McAlpine	19
Jamie Doyle	19
Nicola Lake	20
Katie Viszked	20
Greer Woolley	21
Kelly Neale	21
Sam Wilksch	22
Camilla Jameson	22
Rachael Gray	23
Isobel Smith	24
Jennifer Ainsworth	24
Jazmin Carter	25
Melinda Mabbutt	26
Bethan Jelf	26
Emma McLean	27
Martin Higgins	27
Rosie Spragg	28
Jennifer Tierney	28
Leanne White	29
Rebecca Colby	29
Briony Ashcroft	30
Lisa Gowin	30
Cheryl Jenkinson	31
Dale Clarke	31
Danielle Simons	32
Katrina Turzynski	32
Steve Holt	33
Amy Chaplin	33
Joshua Higgs	34
Jason Hinton	34
Natalie Finch	35
Martika Rumble	35
Letitia Hogston	36
Hannah Franklin	36
Jennifer Roney	37
Nicola Springer	38
Katherine Scott	38

James Thompson	39
Susie Miller	40
Sarah Leeson	40
Greg McBirney	41
Amy Waller	42
Sarah Bradley	42
Kim Calvé	43
Georgina Smith	43

Carrington Middle School

Holly Roper	44
Charlotte Buckley	44
Tamsin Greaves	45
Jonathan Buckley	45
Katie Feeney	46
David Bushrod	47
Lorna Evans	48

Claytons Combined School

George Burkitt	49
Jack Cooper	50
Lee Togwell	50
Emma Quin	51
Euan Thomas	52
Carl Mitch	52
Lisa Darrah	53

Green Park Combined School

Dominic Hillman	53
Ann Darvill	54
Stuart Atkinson	54
Thomas Perry	55
Lianne Redman	55
Aaron Wrigley	56
Claire Taylor	56
Melanie Carter	56

Kerry Campbell	57
Lauren Thrussell & Hannah Barklamb	57
Sarah Gooden	58
Zoë Langridge	58
Matthew Osborne	58
Lauren Holmes	59
Laura Howe	59
Juliet Aldridge	60
Nicholas Onan-Read & Lee Cahill	60
Alison Ings	61
Laura Bottoms	61
Joanne Jenkins	62
Becky Loake	62
David Brooks	63
Sarah & Kayleigh Hurley	63
James Chaplin	63
Nicholas Webb	64
Libby Gray	64
Laura Kirkland	65
Steven Moseley	65
Debbie McCaffrey & Joanne Cahill	66
David Murray	67
Mohsin Hashmi	67
Rebecca Sharman	68
Joanne Westwood	68
Murray Forrest	69
Jason Peters	69
James Hunt	69
Samantha Bates & Emma Barklamb	70
Emma Barklamb	70
Gemma Rainey	71
Chris Kendall	71
Niki Tibble	71
Michelle Cole	72
Kelly Redman & Laura Bottoms	72
Shane Shah	73

Gemma Fretwell	73
Kimberley Harvey	74
Katie Nelson	75
Oliver Gordon	75
Lily Martin	76

Grenville Combined School

Chrissy Bunyan	76
Claire Bunyan	77

High March School

Nicole Abdul	77
Jennifer Nicolaison	78
Natasha Cleland	78
Alexandra Wain	79
Emma Hopkins	79
Lauren Carter	79
Charlotte Matthews	80
Clare Conway	80
Laura Young	80
Ravneek Cheema	81
Sara Salehian	81
Rebecca Duncan	82
Emma Horn	82
Emily Watson	83
Lucy Blake	83
Lisa Rust	84
Lizzie Heeley	84
Emily Green	85
Lottie Greenhow	85
Veronika Riedl	86
Louise Bralsford	86
Katy Bell	87
Rachel Harris	88
Sarah Ratner	88
Louise Hatton	89
Elizabeth Andrew	89

Cassie Macleod	90
Emily Halley	90
Jane Fuerst	90
Amy Duncan	91
Caroline Carter	91
Sophie Burness	91
Genevieve Watson	92
Lizzie Trott	92
Claira Evans	92
Lucie Stangl	93
Charlotte Rees	93
Claire Field	94
Lauren Fitzpatrick	94
Clare Thomas	94
Carolyn Eaton	95
Sarah Filler	95
Nicola Jones	96
Gemma Bradshaw	96

High Wycombe CE Combined School

Jane Ashby	96
Katy Thompsett	97
Anna Lancaster	98
Elizabeth Hoyle	98
Aaron Henry	99
Tom Davies	100

Holy Trinity CE County Middle School

Sophie Binks	100
Luke Hudson	101
Jack Guttery	101
Hazel Inniss	101
Sam Turner	102
Luke Godfrey	102

Jade Knowlden	102
Christian Foy	103
Kelly Weston	103
Phillip Bryant	104
Francesca Randall	104
Faye Devereux	105
Kayleigh Melling	105
Amy Foskett	105

Lent Rise School

Leanne Oxlade	106
Zoe Austin	107
Lauren Austin	108
Michael Burfoot	108
Jack Groves	109
Katie Bisgrove	109
Tommy Clifford	110
Christopher David Argrave	110
Emma Anderton	111
Nicholas Kennedy	111
Gemma Campbell	112
Daniel Russell	112
Matthew Fenwick	113
Lauren Russell	113

Long Crendon C Combined School

Aidan Williams	114
Sarah Martin	114
Andrew Cameron	115
Kristian Purchase	116
Laura Hastings	117
Rosanna Ryan	118
Amy Smith	119
Vicki Osborne	119
Catherine Maxwell	120
Lauren Michael	120
Natalie Barnes	121

	Hannah Young	122
	Becky Hamment	122
	James Pepper	123
	Alison Penford	124
	Francesca Tonkin	125

Malman's Green School

	Katharine Langridge	125
	Sarah Carter	126
	Nikki Reale	126
	Laura Fedorciow	127
	Elizabeth Jenkins	127
	Michaela Hunt	128
	Sarah Scott	128
	Candice Miles	129
	Amy De Marsac	129
	Jenna Herbert	130
	Anneka Crawley	131
	Tara Brocklehurst	132
	Anneka Patel	133
	Louisa Franks	134
	Emma Nowell	134
	Katharine Head	135
	Robyn Sutcliffe	135
	Nicole Robin	136
	Robyn Malpass	136
	Emilie Hawker	137
	Maryam Rafique	138
	Olivia Cairns	138
	Kiri Clarke	139
	Sarah Niven	139
	Jenny Hall	140
	Elizabeth Wynne-Ellis	140
	India Bryant	141
	Chloe Bristow	142
	Reena Rai	143

Amy Appleby	143
Danielle Read	144
Victoria Marsh	145
Alexandra Lewis	146
Emily Dimmock	147
Rebecca Fry	147
Olivia Boniface	148
Emily Dillon	149
Fiona Levey	150
Claire Roberts	151

Oak Green CM School

Liam Gibbins	151
Elle Angelo	151
Jade Spurden	152
David Brown	152
Luke Baughan	153
Jade Maginn	153
Jade Harley	154
Carly Brooks	154
Catherine Haedicke	155
Jemma Galley	155
Alexandra Best	156
Kayleigh Butler	156
Shane Richards	157
Emma Hutchinson	157
Amber Jayne Cawkwell	158
Shahrzad Souidi	158
Kylie Downie	159
Shazia Begum	159
Caroline Lacey	160
Rebecca Campbell	160
Charlotte Murney	161
Ross Newman	161
Dominique Davis	162
Sarah Mumford	162

	Matthew Alderton	163
	Emma Downer	164
	Leanne Coleman	164
	Stephen Brown	165
	Mark Thurley	165

Olney Middle School

Hollie McEvoy	166
Alice Shepherd	166
Graham Terry	167
Alice Croxford	168
Joel Borkin	168
Emily Evans	169
Charlotte Inchbald	169
Charlotte Hathaway	170
Laura Wilkes	170
Natalia Valverde	171
Liam Shane Stewart	171
Amy Allen	172
Charlotte Avery	172
Sarah Barr	173
Rebecca Brown	173
Jessica Small	174
Darren Page	174
Lucy Hoten	175
Paul Andrews	175
Natalie Batchelor	176
Jonathan Lucas	176
Charlotte Abraham	176
Vicki Ibbett	177
Victoria Mountford	177
Zoë Jupp	178
Nicholas Carter	178
Lauren Smith	179
Andy Mason	179
Rebecca Partridge	180

Mark James	180
Nicholas Fitzgerald	181
Kelly Scowen	181
Alice Lambe	182
Amy Ward	182
Eilidh Potter	183
Lauren Shkurko	183
Alexander Burchmore	184
Tristan Derry	184

St Augustine's RC Combined School, High Wycombe

Dario Smith	184
Natasha Wort	185
Martin Fox-Clinch	186
Kasia Markowska	186
Matthew Watson	186
Helen Sherwood	187
Iona Sherwood	188
Elyse Langrish	188
Laura Clements	189
Kimberley Alexander	189
Charlotte Williams	190
Iain Davey	190
Natasha Andrews	191
Hannah Harman	191
Samantha Herbert	192
Jane Gleeson	192
Kathryn O'Toole	192
Daniel Da Rocha	193
Charlene Whitmore	193
Daniel McDaid	194
Simon Millbourn	194
Claire Anderson	195

St Mary's CE Combined School, Amersham

Charlotte Toogood	195
Naomi Robertson	196
Victoria Pyle	196

Jenifer Carman-Chart	197
Marieha Mohsin	198
James Bell	199
Sarah Ball	200
Hannah Smith	201
Peter Needs	201
Tania Brannan	202
Tom Gentry	202
James Harper	203
Francesca Lennon	204
Ross Fraser	205
Wendy Phillips	206
Andrew Minton	207
Amy Miles	208

Stokenchurch Middle School

Matthew Smith	208
Graham Hall	209
Melanie Sears	210
Kirsty Rendle	211
Imogen Simmie	212
Thomas Hollis	213
Lara Croxford	214
Kaylie Smith	215
Sarah Webster	216
Harriet Young	217
Rachel Aves	218
Brendan Davis	218
Ben Underwood	219
Heather Bradshaw	220
Paul Nellis	221
Charlotte Horrox	222
James Poulter	223
Aimée Tapson	224
Joanne Hawkins	225

Waterside C C School
- Lauren Farrow — 226
- James Misseldine — 226
- Sabah Ali — 227
- Daniel Thompson — 227
- James Sayers — 227
- Kirsty Scales — 228
- Sam Whitby — 228
- Julie Hopkins — 229
- Darren Hollins & Nathan Miller — 229
- Simon Griffiths — 230
- Gary Bull — 230
- Craig Hill — 231

Willen C C School
- Donna Martin — 231
- Rachel Bayliss — 232
- Samantha Gatehouse — 233
- Helen Thomson — 234
- Mariyah Abbasbhai — 234
- Sarah Jones — 235

William Harding Middle School
- Natasha Aliphon — 236
- Krystal Delaney — 236
- Freya Macknight — 237
- Abi Krzeminski — 237
- Katie Payne & Pippa Coode — 238
- Adam Tansley — 238
- Lisa Housego — 239
- Hayley Yorke & Emily Goodwin — 240

THE POEMS

SPACESHIPS

S ometimes I stand in the stairway but my foot gets stuck in the staircase.
P lanes are scared whenever they see the spaceship.
A liens are scared whenever they see astronauts.
C anes are metal but spaceships are shaped like tin cases.
E at nice soup but aliens eat junk food.
S hips you use in seas but spaceships you use in skies.
H ow could you live in planets, you need special clothes if you don't have them how would you live?
I t's like you are living in the sea because all planets have got is rocks.
P laces like planets, how could you survive, everything will die.
S tay in the spaceship and all you need to do is fly around and have a rest in a spaceship.

Kabir Jahan (10)
Beechview Middle School

MARS AND VENUS

There were two good friends called Mars and Venus,
'Oh no!' They said 'It's seen us! It's seen us!'
I'll give you a clue, it's hot, but doesn't blow,
It stays in one big place you know!

I hope you've guessed it, the great big sun.
Mars escaped, while Venus ate a bun!
We saw a planet called Lovely Bear,
We know what we saw, shall we take you there?

We're going home, we've had enough of this,
We're not coming back here to get a burn like a kiss!

Adeyinka Ogunekun (10)
Beechview Middle School

PLANETS

Nine planets let's take a look at what the aliens do,
On Mercury it's so hot all the aliens are red,
but they still want a tan!
On Venus as the Romans' Goddess of Love,
the aliens are having a kiss and a cuddle!
On Earth, the aliens are busy, weird and horrible!
On Mars the aliens think they're royal, eating chocolate bars.
On Jupiter the aliens are looking at their big red spot
On Saturn the aliens are playing on the rings
around and around having fun!
On Uranus the aliens are cold and blue, they are suffering from the flu.
On Neptune the aliens are even colder, but still play all day.
On Pluto they sit and watch the Disney channel in their little beds.

Kylie Twitchen (9)
Beechview Middle School

SPACE

When I go to space,
I have to pack my suitcase,
I feel I am in a race.

When I go near the sun,
I feel I am as hot as a bun,
I feel I weigh a ton.

When I go to Mars,
I feel like a star,
I'd rather go in my car.

Siobhan Miles (9)
Beechview Middle School

A Day In Space

3, 2, 1 off we go.
Up in the sky
where the clouds are floating high.

Finally we reach the stars
I feel like I'm floating on Mars,
and over there I see the sun
space is just so much fun.

I can't wait to tell the girls and boys
'When you're in space you don't need toys.
There is just so much to see
so come and fly with me.

Don't worry about your pocket money
space is actually quite funny.
So all you have to do is say the word
and you'll be flying like a bird.'

Katie Marmion (9)
Beechview Middle School

Space

The one thing I hate about space,
is because all the planets are in a race,
I think the aliens come from Mars,
but to me they look like grandpas,
I think I know what's driving over the stars,
Maybe it could be the aliens' cars,
The spaceship from Saturn,
makes wonderful patterns.
Space is just one big maze,
and I think space is a terrible craze.

Charlotte Farmer (10)
Beechview Middle School

OUT OF THIS WORLD!

There are nine planets in the Milky Way.
This is a mouthful to say
Especially in the middle of May.

My favourite planet is Neptune.
If you don't like it you're a total loon.
They say there'll be a comet soon.
In June.
It will come from the moon.

The comet's arrived.
There's a little face peeking outside
He should have eaten a rocket,
They give you a nice ride.

Sukhwinder K Banser (10)
Beechview Middle School

MARS AND JUPITER

Mars and Jupiter had a fight.
In the great big starry night.
Mars was winning two to one,
When along came the enormous sun.
'What are you doing?' The sun cried.
'I'm playing with Jupiter' Mars lied.
'No you're not you're having a fight,
right here in the middle of the night.
Well now's the time to stop the fun
go home, run, run, run' screamed the sun.
And do you know what?
To this day Mars and Jupiter never came out to play.

Rochelle Williams (10)
Beechview Middle School

UP IN SPACE

Space is long and dark,
Like our local park.
It has green men flying around up there,
I bet the spaceships will give you a scare.
There is the moon with craters in,
Much more deeper than your garden bin.
Comets fly quickly round,
Quicker than a greyhound.
There is Saturn with a misty ring around.
Jupiter is the biggest planet I have found,
Pluto is a freezing planet,
It is also in a cartoon.
Mars is the red planet,
It is near our moon.
That is all I have to tell.
Oh look,
There goes the school bell.

Paul Galbraith (10)
Beechview Middle School

IN SPACE

In space there are lots of stars like Mars,
Which is another form of chocolate bars,
Saturn has rings all around, even when you're upside down,
Jupiter is the largest planet in space,
With its red-hot surface that burns your face.
Pluto is the smallest planet in the solar system
And it's the coldest, but not the oldest,
These are some of the planets in space.

Sara Asady (10)
Beechview Middle School

TOUR OF THE PLANETS

I was playing in my garden, just the other day,
It must have been about the end of May,
Then *zap!* An alien appeared in a spaceship,
He had three eyes and a big green lip.

He or she was four feet high,
He or she had a huge sigh,
He offered me a trip to the moon,
I really thought he was a loon!

But then I found he was sincere,
Inside I found was full of fear,
He managed to persuade me,
That I could live quite happily.

I saw a lot on this tour,
Planets, stars and many more!
Mercury, Venus, Earth and Mars,
A million and one tiny stars.

There's Jupiter, Saturn, Uranus too,
The aliens on Neptune have the flu,
And last but not least, Pluto's left,
Apparently he's full of theft.

We went back home at the end of the day,
Boy! It's been a busy Sunday
I went to the kitchen for something to eat,
I was in time for Coronation Street!

Kerry Norwood (10)
Beechview Middle School

WHEN I WENT TO MARS

One rainy day
must have been in May
I was doing my homework
when in my garden I saw
a spaceship land.

I thought I was going mad
but really I was quite sad
what if they wanted to
take me away.

'We come in peace' I heard them say
but in bed quite still I lay.

I decided to go out of the house
but I thought I saw a mouse
I was about to scream
but someone gave me ice-cream
so it shoved it in my mouth.

Up in space we went
how boiling hot Mercury was
how freezing cold Mars is.

Mars is boring
Mars is dull
Mr Mars I want to go home.

I flew in a rocket back to Earth
there I saw my parents once more.

Gemma Giadom (9)
Beechview Middle School

SPACE

Asteroids and astronauts are in space.
The sun and stars are in space.
The moon and Mars are in space.
Pluto and other planets are in space.
Space, space, space, space.

Rockets rocketing in space.
Aliens attacking in space.
Saturn spinning in space
Ships shooting in space
Space, space, space, space.

Earth and Mars spin so fast.
Saturn and Jupiter spin with a ring.
The sun is a star and doesn't spin far
All the planets will spin
But stars like the sun don't begin.
Space, space, space, space.

Timmy Lavelle (9)
Beechview Middle School

SPACE

Up in space, flying around,
Stopping at Saturn, eating bits of Mars.
Turning Neptune on and dancing around.
Buying Mercury trainers to hop and jump about.
Saying 'Hi' to Pluto and patting him on the back.
That's the planets up in space.

Jasmine White (9)
Beechview Middle School

SPACE

What will be in space?
Aliens with tails!
How will they get there?
On the back of hump-back whales!

Why will they be there?
Because they like the dark!
What will they eat there?
A multicoloured shark!

How long have they been there?
Are they very small?
How did I get there?
I haven't been at all!

Neil Johnston (10)
Beechview Middle School

COSMIC

Black holes and meteors,
planets and the moon
rockets and astronauts are going
to meet them soon.

The rockets take off and go
up into space,
the astronauts are strapped down
from their head to their waist.

They look out of the window
and see the bright moon ahead,
and while this is going on
we're back on Earth in bed.

James Hollings (12)
Bierton CE Combined School

COSMIC

In the clear blue sky up in space
The comets and planets are having a race,
Racing around the stars, racing past the sun
Comet and planet racing is so much fun.

The stars shine so bright
Twinkling all the night,
I look up to the sky and I can see
Pluto, Neptune and Mercury.

As we travelled through space
The moon's gleaming, silver face
Glowed so bright,
All through the night.

As we were ending our journey through the night
A comet flew by and gave us a fright.
We travelled back to earth in the moonlight
And we felt it was a really good night!

Emma Ward (12)
Bierton CE Combined School

COSMIC

M ars is the red planet,
E arth is roughly the same size.
R acing around the sun,
C omets and meteorites are flying past.
U ranus is a green planet,
R ings surround it,
Y et it is not the furthest planet of them all.

Hayley Morris (12)
Bierton CE Combined School

Cosmic

Round and round the planet Mars,
In, out through all the stars.

I like driving my rocket in space,
Beating aliens in every race.

In fact I'm in a race right now,
The end is at the Plough.

My best mate is a little green man,
He is the greatest, I'm his favourite fan.

I'm driving very fast, but he's right on my tail
He built his rocket with a hammer and nail.

But I'm nearly there, I made it to the finish line
I've won the aliens' race of all time.

Adam Llewellyn (11)
Bierton CE Combined School

Cosmic

Galaxies and nebulae
It's a space spectacular.
Mars and Jupiter,
The sun and Mercury.
I like to see.

In outer space, there's no human race,
But each and every alien, has an ugly face
Lunar craters and big stars,
Big red giants and Earth and Mars.

Kristian Purdie (12)
Bierton CE Combined School

COSMIC

Looking out of the glass
Watching all the things go past,
I can see Neptune round and blue
I can see Uranus and Pluto too.

Pluto is small as small as can be
That is why it is hard to see,
Uranus is very green,
It is the third planet I have seen.

The sun shines so, so bright
And gives our planet plenty of light,
The sun gives off many rays
And because of the sun we have night and day.

Jupiter has a big red spot
And many moons it has got,
Mars is only very small
In a shape of a small, red ball.

There is Saturn with its rings
They are made of rocks and things,
I can see Earth, it's green and blue
With white, fluffy clouds surrounding it too.

Julia Padget (12)
Bierton CE Combined School

COSMIC

Spaceman
Spaceman
Come and fly with me
I know about you and the planets
So come and see where I've been
I know you're keen!

Spaceman
Spaceman
I know where you've been
I want to show you all my dreams
So come and fly with me.

Thomas Simonds (11)
Bierton CE Combined School

Cosmic

Up, up, up I go into space,
Trying to find an alien race.

I will look everywhere from Mercury to Mars,
Maybe they're on Saturn or playing in the stars.

Will they be red and spotty?
Or will they just be green?
Will they be blue and dotty?
Or will they just be cream?

I wonder if they'll be small,
Or big and round and fat,
I wonder if they'll be tall,
And wear a large top hat.

Do you think that they'll be slimy,
Or do you think that they'll be smooth,
Do you think that they'll look grimy,
And will they be able to move?

Now wait just a minute, I think I can see one,
Yes I can, no wait, it's my mum!

Sarah Cosby (12)
Bierton CE Combined School

Cosmic

As I look out through the window of my spacecraft,
I see silvery stars gleaming down on me.
The sun's hot rays dazzling my face.
A red warm planet called Mars.
Now we're approaching Saturn the colossal ringed planet.
Big green Uranus is a sight to be seen,
twinned with Neptune which is watery-blue.
Here comes giant, stormy, red-eyed Jupiter,
dwarfing poor distant tiny Pluto.
Mercury, the two-faced planet is now in sight,
one side hot, one side cold a most extraordinary planet to behold.
The moon's pockmarked surface, the glowing light,
the way it does on Earth at night.
Last but not least, Earth,
but in my opinion it is the best
I think Earth outshines the rest!

Nicola Evans (11)
Bierton CE Combined School

Cosmic

All the planets far out in space
All orbiting round the sun in a race,
Mercury first and Pluto last
And the millions of stars pass.

Soon, we on Earth will be coming second
But the silly old moon said a horrid word,
So Mars zoomed off and we were still in third,
Then a meteor knocked us off course.

We were coming third at the speed of a bird,
All the planets took wrong positions,
So the sun got angry - he went mad!
Mercury came first, how sad.

Christopher Crawford (11)
Bierton CE Combined School

COSMIC

Out into the night as far as the eye
could see,
Past the moon and the Sea of Tranquillity.

I reported back to NASA, the space station,
That I could spot a star constellation.

Travelling at speed but getting very fast,
With Jupiter and Venus going past.

Flying past are so-called 'shooting stars',
Past little Pluto, Uranus and Mars.

There goes a rather unusual planet,
Made of rock, water, stone and granite.

There's the sun with its red-hot core,
Which gives us energy and a whole
lot more.

So we turned back to Earth and the
human race,
But I really enjoyed my mission into
space.

Charlotte Handy (12)
Bierton CE Combined School

Cosmic

I can see Mars,
I can see the stars,
In my space rocket
I have a spacesuit with a pocket.

I go out in it,
And I nearly had a fit,
When a shooting star came by,
And nearly hit my eye.

But I can still see Jupiter,
I think that it is supiter.
The moon is really weird,
The man on it has a beard.

Some of the other planets,
Are really just like granite
Except for Saturn with the rings,
Which are made with many things.

Pluto is very cold,
And also very old.
I can see an alien
Whose English was a failure.

That's all I can remember,
From that time in September,
When I went to fly,
Up above the sky.

Annabel Vooght (11)
Bierton CE Combined School

Cosmic

I can see the twinkly stars,
I can see the Earth's own moon,
I can see a huge, brown meteorite
Landing on Earth very soon.

I can see the fiery comets,
I can see ancient, red Mars,
I can see a huge, brown meteorite
Faster than the fastest cars.

I can see the strangest asteroids,
I can see my friend, Alien Zed,
I can see a huge, brown meteorite
That hit me on the head.

Emma Piotrowski (11)
Bierton CE Combined School

Cosmic

As I fly up into space,
It seems a dark and scary place.

As I journey through twinkling stars,
I see green Earth and bright red Mars.

I see shiny Saturn and the sparkling sun,
This journey's becoming really fun.

As I go through the Milky Way
I can see home, millions of miles away.

I finally fall back to the ground,
And will soon speak of everything I found.

Hannah Scrimshaw (11)
Bierton CE Combined School

Cosmic

Saturn, Jupiter, Venus and Mars,
Uranus and Pluto and shooting stars.
The sun and the Earth and the moon in the sky,
The astronauts in rockets that fly up real high.
The stars are shining, shining so bright,
Twinkling and blinking and giving off light.
The moon is dull and really grey,
And always comes out at the end of the day.
The sun is hot and makes us feel warm,
And always rises at the beginning of dawn.
I see little green men on the planet Mercury,
They have no eyes so they cannot see.
I see two rockets having a race,
Out of Earth and into space.

Lorna Kelleher (12)
Bierton CE Combined Schools

Cosmic

I am in my rocket proud as can be
In the big universe, there's lots to see
The stars, the planets and the sun
Which is so hot you could toast a hot cross bun.

I am going on forever and ever, I'm never going to stop,
Oh! I have landed on a planet, I wish there was a shop.
I see a green thing, then I realise it's an alien man
Running to a van.

I am scared, there is no one here.
I would like to go back home and everyone would cheer,
I wish very hard that I could be back home in my bed,
And before I know it, I am back and dreaming of the adventure I led.

Amanda Young (11)
Bierton CE Combined School

Cosmic

Wow Mum! That's cosmic,
I'm going round my friend's house,
he just made a smooth move next door
and his Dad's got an RS Turbo.
Wow Mum! That's cosmic,
I just got a new bike,
it's got smooth moves
and looks like an RS Turbo.
Wow Mum! That's cosmic,
I just joined a new band,
I think I made a smooth move
and the band leader's got an RS Turbo.
Wow Mum! That's cosmic,
you just bought a doughnut maker,
well that is a smooth move,
did you go in your RS Turbo?
Whoa Dad! That's not cosmic,
you forgot the petrol,
now that's not a smooth move
and the RS Turbo's broken down.

Richard McAlpine (12)
Bourton Meadow Combined School

Cosmic

I was speeding through the sparkling stars
in my turbo cosmic rocket halfway through the galaxy.

I was floating through the sparkling stars
on my turbo cosmic cruiser boat halfway through the galaxy.

I was flying through the sparkling stars
on my turbo cosmic space car halfway through the galaxy.

Jamie Doyle (12)
Bourton Meadow Combined School

Cosmic!

I saw the planets whirling,
    at a speedy pace.
I saw the dark, gloomy universe,
    in the night sky.
I saw the lacy stars,
    shining on my face.
I saw a dark, black hole,
    just passing by.
I saw the galaxy open,
    for me to see the light.
I have seen it all now,
    so for now good night.

Nicola Lake (11)
Bourton Meadow Combined School

Cosmic

Speeding through the galaxy
On my spaceship Kat
Flying through the universe
On my rocket . . . Splat

Speeding through the galaxy
Crashing on Mars
Bumping up and down
Flying through the stars

Speeding through the galaxy
On my spaceship Kat
Flying through the universe
On my rocket . . . Splat.

Katie Viszked (11)
Bourton Meadow Combined School

Cosmic

In a pure black sky, on a dark warm night,
The stars are twinkling so high and so bright.
Then the moon in the corner, a smooth tinted white,
An oval gleaming sphere.
The sun is setting now the beautiful colours I see as I peer.
The galaxy lovely wonders but when does it end?
We will only know when a rocket we will send.
The planets all around us but why do we not see.
I do not understand it is such a wonder to me.
The comet now speeding over the sky.
Over the horizon it does fly.
All questions but just no answers.
Why?
I will never know.

Greer Woolley (11)
Bourton Meadow Combined School

Cosmic

Cosmic I'm flying through space
In my supersonic ship.
Cosmic I'm in the Milky Way
Past all the satellites and whatever else is there.
Cosmic I'm passing all the stars
With their blinding blue light and millions there are.

Cosmic I've met an alien
All green bumpy and round
Cosmic the alien he is not
He is chasing me away
Cosmic I'm in my supersonic ship
I start the engine away I go.

Kelly Neale (12)
Bourton Meadow Combined School

COSMIC

'Dad, what does cosmic mean?'
'Well, it means:
Turbo rushing supersonic,
Bubbly drinks, all alcoholic.
Rockets flying outer space,
Gonna find another race.'

'Mum, what does cosmic mean?'
'Well, it means:
A kind of, sort of exclamation,
A human headed pink Dalmatian.
Aliens running about on Mars,
Small red dwarfs, and shooting stars.'

'Grampy, what does cosmic mean?'
'Well, it means:
Mars Bars and Milky Ways,
Alien intergalactic days.
Blinding stars, the speed of light,
The brightness of day, and the darkness of night.'

'Gran, are you cosmic?'

Sam Wilksch (11)
Bourton Meadow Combined School

THE COSMIC ATMOSPHERE!

I plunged my rocket into the cosmic atmosphere,
The sun was falling, and the moon was nearly here.
The stars were twinkling in the dark night sky,
A bright, fast shining comet whizzed by.

My rocket landed on the surface of Mars,
I looked up above, and saw millions of stars.
The ground was brown, dusty and cold
Don't go too far, I had been told.

I found a gold gem, oh please don't let me drop it,
I explored a bit further than ran to my rocket.
Up into the atmosphere, I did fly,
Swallowed up by a black mass, a kind of sky.

It's nearly time to go, I've been here quite a while,
As I fly past all the planets, my face lights up a smile.
I plunge out of the cosmic atmosphere,
The moon was falling, and the sun was nearly here.

Camilla Jameson (11)
Bourton Meadow Combined School

COSMIC

Up there in that
black dull place
there's spacey stuff
out of this world.
Look there's a bright
ball of fire over
there quick a dash
a dash of light
a comet flying right
past my nose.
The gleaming bright stars
making shapes
in the dark black sky
and there it is
the moon itself
like it's glowing
in the dark.
The planets surrounding
the sun are just
as mysterious as them all.

Rachael Gray (7)
Bourton Meadow Combined School

COSMIC

Sun, sun glorious sun
Please shine down on me
You are so very bright
That you make me blind
Blind, blind, blind.

Sun, sun glorious sun
I look up at you
You are so very bright
I cannot stand the light
Light, light, light.

Sun, sun glorious sun
I love you very much
That you can be there
On Monday for a sunny day
Day, day, day.

Sun, sun glorious sun
You are so bright in the sky
At night the moon shines bright
In the morning you come out and shine
Shine, shine, shine.

Isobel Smith (8)
Bourton Meadow Combined School

HEAVEN KNOWS

We see the galaxy far beyond,
Heaven knows what's lying there.
We see the stars up, up and away,
Heaven knows what they're doing there.
We see the planets lying there,
Heaven knows what's on them.

We see the speed that rockets go,
Heaven knows how fast they are.
We see the alien on planet Mars,
Heaven knows how it got there.
We see the land on Planet Earth,
Heaven knows how we got there!

Jennifer Ainsworth (12)
Bourton Meadow Combined School

COSMIC

The teacher's voice buzzes in my ear
One minute till half-past three
I can see the rocket landing
No one else can.

The bell goes I'm so excited
I think I'll go to Mars today
and Jupiter tomorrow.

I'm turning to an alien
To go and meet my friends
Pen and paper ready
to translate to them again.

I'm going home now
It's half-past five
My dinner will be ready
See you in years to come.

The teacher's voice buzzes in my ear
One minute till half-past three
I can see the rocket landing
No one else can.

Jazmin Carter (11)
Bourton Meadow Combined School

A Child's Cosmic Questioning

Are there aliens on Mars,
Do they drive little cars?
Are there any men in green,
Do they look like a runner bean?

Mars is red, purple and pink,
Do these men have a sink?
Where do they wash, where do they clean,
Do they have soap or Mr Sheen?

I wish I could go to Mars,
Or explore some other stars.
Are there any aliens out there,
If so, then where?

Melinda Mabbutt (12)
Bourton Meadow Combined School

Cosmic!

We are shooting through space
at turbo speed.
We've passed Mars and Jupiter
and shot through Saturn's rings.
We are on course for Pluto
Just one more planet to go.
We are on a crash course
heading straight for Pluto.
We're going to have to land,
but hopefully there is sand.
We have hit! Bad luck!
Oh no! I can't breathe.
Beam me up Scotty!
Dinner time.

Bethan Jelf (11)
Bourton Meadow Combined School

COSMIC

In the darkness of the sky
I saw shooting stars go by
Faster than a rocket faster than a plane
I saw shooting stars go by
By, by, by.

In the darkness of the sky
I saw shooting stars go by
Whizzing here and whizzing there
Around the planets in the night
I saw shooting stars go by
By, by, by.

In the darkness of the sky
I saw shooting stars go by
Silently dying away
In the darkness of the sky
I saw shooting stars go by
By, by, by.

Emma McLean (8)
Bourton Meadow Combined School

DAAAD!

Daaad what does cosmic mean?
Well my boy it means '*Mmm* let me think,
aaa I got it, oh no!
I haven't now
I've definitely got it now
It means I'm descending
to outer space to find another race.'

Martin Higgins (12)
Bourton Meadow Combined School

COSMIC

Cosmic Cosmic
Cosmic powers

Cosmic Cosmic
out to Mars

Cosmic Cosmic
out in space

Cosmic Cosmic
in a different place

Cosmic Cosmic
in a different world

Cosmic Cosmic
what a wonderful word.

Rosie Spragg (8)
Bourton Meadow Combined School

COSMIC!

Rocketing through space,
on a turbo Cosmic race,
with an alien space-race!

Oh no! They've hit a satellite,
on this turbo cosmic flight,
what a terrible plight!

The only thing I need
is a turbo rocket full of speed
on this turbo Cosmic flight
with the aliens in sight!

Jennifer Tierney (12)
Bourton Meadow Combined School

CLASPS OF DEATH

The galaxy's free from violence, the silence
is broken by the sound of a gun.
A gun being shot by a victorious soldier,
sharing his joy with the galaxy.
That soldier is free,
The galaxy's free,
Free from the clasps of death.

The peace was shattered, people scattered
To take shelter from the bombs and noise.
Voices crying,
People dying,
Dying in the
Clasps
Of
Death.

Leanne White (10)
Bourton Meadow Combined School

COSMIC

The stars are yellow and shine
bright and twinkle,
The sun shines down on us,
The stars are glowing,
The moon is white and watching
us from the blue deep sky,
I wish I could see all the
twinkling stars and see the moon
that watches us and see the
sun shine bright.

Rebecca Colby (7)
Bourton Meadow Combined School

Cosmic

When I came to Mars
I saw a load of stars
Then came the monster of Mars
And ate all the stars

I said stop!
But it went pop
Then I said bye
And it said why?

When I got back
I went black
The monster had followed
Me back!

Briony Ashcroft (7)
Bourton Meadow Combined School

Cosmic

As I travelled through space
A shooting star I faced

I reached out high to touch the star
But I didn't reach very far

I tried and tried again and again
I tried and tried until I cried
I tried one last time
The shooting star I never did claim

So I cried, cried, cried.

Lisa Gowin (8)
Bourton Meadow Combined School

COSMIC

When I went to Mars
I ate some chocolate bars.
Then I ate some stars
And then a Milky Bar.

The moon the moon looks
Like an egg on a spoon.
The moon the moon is
Made out of rock but
An egg is not.

The sun the sun is like
A round hot cross bun.
The sun the sun is a
Ball of fun.

Cheryl Jenkinson (8)
Bourton Meadow Combined School

COSMIC

In outer space,
Is there a different race?
Stars shine so bright,
Would they give you a fright?
The night sky far away
Would aliens find their way?
Other planets miles away
Would you like to visit one, one day?
The stars are beautiful at night
I would love to visit one, one night
That's cosmic my son, space far away.

Dale Clarke (12)
Bourton Meadow Combined School

COSMIC

Star, moon.
I look up at the sky
I look at that great big star.
Lovely sun shining nice.
Lovely moon twinkling bright
I'll see you tomorrow night.

Star, moon.
I look up at you.
You are the best thing for night.
I see you twinkling bright
I look at you all night.
I'll see you tomorrow night.

Star, moon.
I look up at the great Milky Way.
It is great to look at it.
You are looking at me.
I'll see you tomorrow night.

Danielle Simons (7)
Bourton Meadow Combined School

COSMIC

In space there's a spaceman
In a space world he has a space dog
who eats space meat

He has a space cat who eats space mice
The space mice run away well some of them do

He has a space bird who eats up all the space seeds
so the other birds can't eat some as well.

Katrina Turzynski (7)
Bourton Meadow Combined School

What A Cosmic Day

One day I went to a theme park and I had a cosmic day
in every way.
I went on a roller-coaster but I admit
I am a bit of a boaster.
One day I went to a theme park and I had a cosmic day
in every way.
I went on the swings and I felt I had wings.
One day I went to a theme park and I had a cosmic day
in every way.
I went on the rocket ride but it was actually a slide.
One day I went to a theme park and I had a cosmic day
in every way.
I went on the alien ride it was worse than that
silly old slide.
One day I went to a theme park and I had a cosmic day
in every way.
I went on the log flume and it took
me for a real zoom.
One day I went to a theme park and I had a cosmic day
in every way.

Steve Holt (11)
Bourton Meadow Combined School

Cosmic

Twinkling stars in the sky
I wish I could be up there with them
They shine so bright in the sky
The Milky Way like a chocolate bar
Is still there in the sky
Shining brightly in our eyes
But is it there right now?

Amy Chaplin (7)
Bourton Meadow Combined School

COSMIC

Shooting stars go shooting up into space
I feel like they touch my face
They run away so fast
I can't even catch them
When they go past.

Rockets go out in space
Before they go to base
They have seen the moon
It is like a silver spoon.

Up in the sky
I see the stars
They are so, so bright
Glittering in space.

Joshua Higgs (7)
Bourton Meadow Combined School

COSMIC

Turbo cosmic smooth move
up we go up to space
in our RS Turbo rocket.
We have to go to a smooth moon
with little green men running around
they look a little like marshmallows
and they have little smiling faces
and long tentacles.
So we speed off in our RS Turbo rocket
back to Earth.
Home at last where I had my birth.

Jason Hinton (12)
Bourton Meadow Combined School

Cosmic

I look up in the sky
It's bright
The stars are flashing in the night
Like a flashing light
Light, light, light.

There's a pattern like a twinkle
The stars are falling from the sky to ground
The sun is the biggest star in the sky.

I see the stars and the moon
Through my telescope
I think when you look through it
It looks closer to me
Me, me, me.

Natalie Finch (7)
Bourton Meadow Combined School

Cosmic

I went to bed and
looked out of
my bed and looked up
up up and at the stars and
they twinkled at me

Twinkle twinkle look at me
I like you and you like me
and twinkle up in the planet up up up in stars
look at the stars
stars stars.

Martika Rumble (8)
Bourton Meadow Combined School

COSMIC

On a dark, starry night,
When the moon is high,
If you listen closely,
You'll hear them gallop by.
Cosmic, silver mane and tail,
She comes to pick me up,
Cosmic, blazing, golden coat,
Picking out the stars.
Flying through the countryside,
At the speed of light,
Flying at the head of the herd,
On a dark, starry night.
Snow sent flying,
By razor sharp hooves,
Manes and tails whipped by the wind,
Flying into my face.
Freezing cold
With ice on the ground,
She's so warm
I don't feel the cold.
Galloping at the speed of light,
We tear up the hills
I whisper the word
'Bella'.

Letitia Hogston (12)
Bourton Meadow Combined School

COSMIC

I have got powers
Magic powers.
I will turn you into a frog
Or a rabbit or if you rather a toad.
No my wizard I'd rather be myself.

I am an alien
I come from a planet called Mars.
I am all green and slimy.
The planet is red and hot.

Hannah Franklin (7)
Bourton Meadow Combined School

COSMIC DREAMS OF SPACE

10 . . . 9 . . . 8 . . . 7 . . . 6 . . . 5 . . . 4 . . . 3 . . . 2 . . . 1
Blast off!
The rocket shoots up,
Into the stars,
But that's just a dream,
Of travelling to Mars.
I climb into bed,
And snuggle up tight,
Time to see the world,
In a different light,
I drift off to sleep,
And in no time at all,
I seem to be on the moon,
And having a ball.
I bounce so high,
I jump onto Mars,
Then I hop onto a shooting star,
(It travels much faster than my Dad's old car)
I see all of space,
It's a different place,
But then I wake up,
As I fall out of bed.
Bump!

Jennifer Roney (11)
Bourton Meadow Combined School

Cosmic

We see the stars in the sky
Up in space, so quiet and deep.
There's millions of those little things
Whizzing around and around.

We see the planets in the sky
But they're far away.
We sometimes see Venus, but maybe not.
Spinning around and around.

We see the sun in the sky
Burning big and bright.
But nothing lives up there,
Burning around and around.

We see the moon in the sky
With the flag upon it.
But we wonder up there if there was life
Circling around and around.

We see the space shuttle in the sky
With the astronauts in it.
The big white thing, with rocket boosters
Blasting around and around.

Nicola Springer (11)
Bourton Meadow Combined School

Cosmic

Milky Way, Milky Way.
You're only made of stars.
Shining bright, shining bright. That's all you do.
Thousands and millions of miles away.

You're so huge not one too many.
Always there not anywhere else.
Always bright, bright, bright.

Katherine Scott (8)
Bourton Meadow Combined School

COSMIC

Shooting through space at warp factor five,
Is the Starship Enterprise.
Kirk at the wheel and Spock at the helm,
They boldly go where no man has gone before!
The ship bends round corners, and rips past Saturn,
Smashing into comets.
They come up to a Romulan battleship,
And the Enterprise is smashed to dust!
Wait, smashed to dust, the Enterprise,
No way!
Kirk can't die, I'm going to complain to the makers of this film.
I'll read a good book instead.
Now let's see:
Shooting through space at warp factor five,
Is the Starship Enterprise.
Kirk at the wheel and Spock at the helm,
They boldly go where no man has gone before!
They come up on a Klingon battle cruiser and,
Blast it to particles!
That's more like it!
The Enterprise wins!
Dad, do you like Star Trek?
Yes son, it's cosmic!

James Thompson (12)
Bourton Meadow Combined School

Cosmic

I saw a beautiful star in the sky
I wanted to have it but it was too high,
The star was gleaming so beautifully bright
There was just so much glittering light.

A rocket went flying in the sky
It seemed to be going ever so high,
It gave a big shot
It looked so hot
That was the end of my rockedy rock.

The planets were bumping round and round
They kept pushing each other to the ground
There was a big clang
And then a big bang
It started to bend
And that the galaxy came to an end.

Susie Miller (12)
Bourton Meadow Combined School

Cosmic

A bright star in the night
Flashing like a diamond
I look up every night
With my flashing eye eye eye.

The stars are shining
Like a flashing light
In the night night night.

When I look into my telescope
The stars look so close to
Me me me.

The stars will always
Be my favourite thing
In space space space.

Sarah Leeson (8)
Bourton Meadow Combined School

LOOKING FOR A GALAXY

Flying through space to find another galaxy,
It's going to take your brain to another dimension,
We're trying to find another race,
We are going to go into turbo then into hyperspeed,
To find another galaxy!
We're building up to turbo,
We're a blade cutting through space,
With the stars streaming past us and
We're running out of space,
We are going to go into turbo then into
Hyperspeed to find another galaxy!
We're now into hyperspeed,
And we're entering another galaxy,
We've found the alien spaceship and they are
Inviting us in
We are goi . . .
'Peter your tea is ready.'

Greg McBirney (11)
Bourton Meadow Combined School

COSMIC

The stars in the night sky
Shine down on planet Earth.
They twinkle twinkle all night
And never disappear.

They look as shining as a tiny bee.
If you look through a telescope you will see
That they run in and out the sky
And twinkle all night long.

Sparkle, sparkle in the night sky.
Sparkle, sparkle everywhere in the midnight sky.

In the midnight sky shooting stars flying about
Bumping every star in sight.

Amy Waller (8)
Bourton Meadow Combined School

COSMIC

I was travelling along in the deep black sky
When an alien spaceship flew right by
The door flew open, an alien stepped out
It was a big green monster wide and stout.

It said to me
My name is Cosmic
And then with a flick of his jet black wig
He spun around with a little jig.

I fainted right there on the spot
I don't know if Cosmic saw or not
The blood all rushed to my head
Then I found myself back in my bed.

Sarah Bradley (12)
Bourton Meadow Combined School

NEVER-ENDING JOURNEY

Travelling through the velvet
of the never-ending dark,
moving through the galaxy
so quiet and so calm.

Silent through a deep black sea
shoals of stars flew past me.

Quiet through a deep black hole
burrowing through planets like a
soft dark mole.

Travelling through the velvet
of the never-ending dark
moving through the galaxy
so quiet and so calm . . .

Kim Calvé (12)
Bourton Meadow Combined School

COSMIC

Up there in the spacy world
See the astronauts floating round
In the dark with the bright stars.
Even sometimes if you're lucky
One day you might be up there
Floating in the stars and darkness.
You may even spend Christmas there
And you have to open your presents
When you get home because
You may not have a chance in space
Because you may be floating round so much.

Georgina Smith (8)
Bourton Meadow Combined School

MY LIFE IN THE THIRD WORLD

No food, no drink, no clothes to wear,
No money, no house, no place to lay my head.
Sadness and anger, as my life has come this way.
No fun, no joy, no energy to even play.
I have nothing to my name. My family are all dead
And I often wish, I was in heaven, instead.
For days on end, I'll just sit in the burning sun,
I have no future to live for, no need to carry on.
My stomach is empty, I've not eaten for days,
To escape this pitiful life would be like trying to
                         leave a never-ending maze.

Holly Roper (12)
Carrington Middle School

STARLIGHT

The moon has appeared, the sun has gone down
The stars follow him in wonder;
The moon starts to frown
But the stars cheer him up,
With their dazzling dancing parade!
They may be distant planets,
They may be distant suns,
Shining shimmering like a ripple on a beach.
I would love to touch them but they are out of reach.
Oh no, not now, they are starting to fade -
That is the end of the shiny parade.

Charlotte Buckley (12)
Carrington Middle School

CANDLE LIGHT

The candle is burning
Burning so bright
It lights up the room
In the dead of night
The wax is dripping
The candle is wearing low
The light is flaring
With a bright yellow glow
It won't go out
Until I give it a blow
Then off to sleep, I will go.

Tamsin Greaves (12)
Carrington Middle School

SOUNDS OF SILENCE

Have you ever heard the clouds moving?
Or the daisies singing in the breeze?

Do you think you can hear a creeper
Creeping up the wall?
Or the wind blowing through the trees?

Can you hear a bird learning how to fly?
Or the stars flying in the sky?
Or even a spider swinging from leaf to leaf?

No! No! No! Of course not,
These are the sounds of silence.

Jonathan Buckley (8)
Carrington Middle School

SOUNDS OF SILENCE

Have you heard a daisy
swaying in the wind?
Or perhaps a leaf floating
off a tree?
Maybe you have heard a snail
sliding and making his silver trail?
No! These are the sounds of silence.

Can you hear an earthworm
digging up the ground?
Perhaps you've heard a centipede?
No that makes little sound!
Have you heard a hair growing
on your head?
No! These are the sounds of silence.

Maybe you've heard the wind
whispering through the trees?
Or perhaps a foot squelching in the mud?
Can you hear the leaves turning
crisp and brown?
No! No! these are all the sounds of silence!

Katie Feeney (8)
Carrington Middle School

SOUNDS OF SILENCE

Have you ever heard a cat's tail,
swishing in the wind?
Or a centipede taking off its boots?
Or even a ladybird floating
off a leaf?

Have you ever heard a rainbow
being painted on your roof?
Or even a tree,
growing towards the sky?
Or a snake hissing
at the forest?

Have you heard a rabbit
jumping down his hole?
Or even a silkworm
using its silver thread?
Or even a giraffe bending
down with its long neck?
No! These are the sounds of silence!

David Bushrod (8)
Carrington Middle School

SOUNDS OF SILENCE

Have you heard a ladybird
counting all her spots?
Or even a glow-worm showing off its lights?
Or the snow painting its silver shine
on your window?

I want to know if you've heard
the whispers in the wind?
Or have you heard a snail sleeping
in its shell?
Or a caterpillar climbing a tree
and eating a leaf?

Have you heard the sun and
cloud arguing together?
Or have you heard the trees
saying how crooked their arms were?
Or have you heard a little bird making
its nest?
No! No! No! These are the sounds of silence!

Lorna Evans (8)
Carrington Middle School

MY VIRTUAL DOG

My pet dog doesn't ruin my bed,
But its constant beeping rattles my head,
It doesn't eat rotten left-overs from yesterday,
But it totally annoys me in every way.
It drinks cocktails and eats its bowl,
And when it dies it leaves its soul,
I think it's cool before it cries,
But it'll only turn two before it dies.
With the touch of a button footprints vanish
But there is no toilet for it to use.
It likes playing games like catch the ball,
And if you play 'Handshake' I stand so tall.
But if I lose too much I submit to sighs,
And my virtual dog whimpers, if not, cries.
If my virtual pet was real,
I'd have to give it many a meal.
I know I'm not fit to rule,
If it was real it would jump and fall,
I like my dog on its birthday,
'How old is it now' my mum will say.
If I said how old it was - I'd lie,
'Cos my pet dog's guaranteed to die!

George Burkitt (11)
Claytons Combined School

PANSIES ON THE PORCH

Pansies on the porch, dancing in the moonlight
Pansy on the porch, scary through the night
Pansies on the porch, clutch my teddy tight
I turn on my torch
The pansies look towards me
Gasping for light
They're alive!
I dive for the door
I hear my father snore
I cannot take it any more
I go downstairs and search the floor
Behind a cupboard door I found
The weedkiller all safely bound
My mother always said I could hunt like a bloodhound
Squirt now you are dead
All these dancing pansies
Have gone to my head!

Jack Cooper (11)
Claytons Combined School

FOOTBALL

When I shoot it goes so high,
The ball goes up into the sky,
The ball comes down I hit it hard,
I hit it so hard it turned into card,
It just crept into the back of the net,
A dog jumped up and it was my pet.

When I shoot it's like a dart,
It goes too fast as fast as a cart,
When I score I celebrate,
And I celebrate with my mate.

Lee Togwell (9)
Claytons Combined School

THE GHOST LIFT

Once long ago there was a lift
It entered onto three different long dark corridors
Nobody got in or out
Except for ten minutes ago
But for a lift to take ten minutes
to move three floors, it wouldn't
Oh! I shouted then
Ahr! I shouted
I was scared
Boy I was scared
So I rang the bell
But instead a voice said
Ding dong
The bell's just going bong
Bong, bong
Ding, dong
And that
Is the *spooky!* End.

Emma Quin (9)
Claytons Combined School

The Malaboo

The Malaboo has just been spied
By a fisherman who almost died.

It lives on Squash island
In a cave full of slugs and lots of other grim bugs.

The Malaboo eats people
It's thinking of devouring a steeple.

It lurks (ie the monster)
In the depths of the blue sea

The fisherman lost his boat but saved his life
(At least that's the story he told his wife).

Euan Thomas (10)
Claytons Combined School

The Sunset

If the sun did not set
in the evening,
but set
in the morning,
when we come home from school
it would be the beginning
of the day,
and in the morning
we have breakfast
it will be time for bed.

Carl Mitch (12)
Claytons Combined School

THE SPOOKY WOODS!

I was walking in the woods and the wind was blowing,
The stream was fastly flowing,
The leaves were falling,
The owls were calling.

My watch was going 'tick' 'tock' 'tick' 'tock',
It was like the big grandfather clock,
It was so quiet,
Sometimes it was a raging riot!

Lisa Darrah (9)
Claytons Combined School

SERPENT

He lies concealed
As prey approaches.
The unfortunate mouse knew one move
Could destroy his life.
He slithers closer,
Venom dripping from his fangs.
The mouse turns to run,
But gets trapped in the hunter's coil.
Desperate panic sets in -
The mouse is helpless.
Sharp fangs pierce the victim's back
Inserting venom.
Injecting pain.
The snake devours its prey
And continues the hunt.

Dominic Hillman (11)
Green Park Combined School

I Should Like To...

I should like to paint the midnight sky.
The glimmer of moonlight on a frosty night.
I would like to catch the sparkle of a shooting star
and hold it tightly in the palm of my hand.
I should like to paint the sound of silence,
The painter's brush wipes on the canvas.
The sound of the sun as it sinks beneath distant hills.
The mystery surrounding the song of the whales.
I should like to touch the breeze as it whispers
through ancient willow beds,
- secrets of the past, stories for the future.
I hold the key to an unknown world,
hues of frantic colour emerge,
as brush strokes wipe the canvas.

Ann Darvill (10)
Green Park Combined School

Work Of Art

The multi-coloured red arrow soars through the air.
Vivid hues resemble a hand-painted work of art.
It lands at a refuelling station,
Drinking succulent syrup through a long, spiralling straw.
It takes off with vast energy,
Then hovers;
And rests
On nearby vegetation.
It bathes in the sun's warmth
Opening and closing ragged wings,
Respite before the journey towards its far off destination.

Stuart Atkinson (11)
Green Park Combined School

Water Wonder

Clambering up steep shores, searching for
The perfect spot to
Spawn future generations.
Slowly digging,
Creating immense piles of sandy grain
Forming a wondrous wall of
Defence from dangerous predators.

Her agile neck surveys the scene, ready to
Disappear instantly
Into her indestructible helmet.
She peers out of her hiding place
Seeing nothing but land.
Life had deserted the resort,
Allowing her to shuffle safely down the golden beach,
Gracefully swimming away.

Thomas Perry (10)
Green Park Combined School

Night Creature

A dark silhouette obstructs the moon,
Leathery wings flap back and forth,
Concealed in an ebony sky,
Webbed like feet cling desperately to bare branches,
As he hangs,
Viewing the world,
Motionless,
He listens to the dawning of a new day,
Longing for the comforting darkness to continue,
Swiftly he returns to his safe haven,
A paradise of darkness.

Lianne Redman (11)
Green Park Combined School

Red

The brightness of a battlefield
Fighting for a touch of royalty
The broken hearts left behind
Endeavoured in sadness and rage
The sadness of poppies and the
Everlasting sounds are here forever.

Aaron Wrigley (10)
Green Park Combined School

Christmas Cheer

Church bells ring in a far away village,
as children run into tiny cottages.
Songs of joy are heard as the band plays a joyful tune.
Each child wraps up warm, waiting to play in the snow.
The majestic Christmas tree is seen above village rooftops.
Inside a cottage, a Christmas turkey has just come
out of the oven, the smell is rich with flavour.
Laughter of joy is heard as darkness falls upon the village.

Claire Taylor (11)
Green Park Combined School

Baby Shock

Never leave a baby near a socket
Because it could end up going up in a rocket.
There it sits fiddling playing touching
Wires that could be fraying.
Fingers fingers turn it off
So that you won't get a shock.
So never leave your babies near a socket.

Melanie Carter (8)
Green Park Combined School

I Want To Be The Wind

I want to be the north wind,
Competing with the sun,
Losing if I must but I don't want
To run.

        I want to be the south wind,
        Stronger than the rest,
        I know it's silly but I just
        Want to be blessed.

I want to be the east and west,
If I ever could,
I hate to say I'd be a pest, but I know,
I should.

        I want to be the wind
        Sneezing as I go
        I just want to be wind as soft as
        The snow.

Kerry Campbell (11)
Green Park Combined School

Green

The twinkling of the coloured gem,
Lightens up the darkened room,
My face full of envy,
The colour of the delectable fruit
Crunches as I bite,
The sun as it shines through the leaves
Making an emerald glow,
Fresh fields sparkle with dew.

Lauren Thrussell (11) & Hannah Barklamb (10)
Green Park Combined School

Cat

Small, proud creature,
Strolls across the dusty gravel,
Ducking quickly under a bright red car,
Shaded from the sticky sun,
Circling silently,
Settling down,
Curling round and slowly slowly
Dropping off.

Sarah Gooden (10)
Green Park Combined School

The Spider

A light footer
A web maker
A furry creature
A scary monster
A fly catcher
A plughole cover
A night creeper
A good hider.

Zoë Langridge (10)
Green Park Combined School

Waiting

I was waiting,
For your silver netting,
To jump out in front of me.
Leading to your
Famous, fabulous, fly restaurant.

Those competitions,
You won,
Against my family and friends,
Were soon to turn.
I was waiting,
Impatiently waiting.

Matthew Osborne (11)
Green Park Combined School

SPIDER

An eight legger
A fly catcher
A web winder
A light footer
A spine chiller
A fast scuttler
A hole lover
A crack creeper
A human frightener.

Lauren Holmes (11)
Green Park Combined School

I SHOULD LIKE TO

I should like to paint the magic in
a well-loved story,
I would like to see the wind as it whistles
through straining trees,
I should like to glimpse the dark side of the moon,
And catch a shimmering star,
I would like to touch the furthest planet,
And understand the meaning of life.

Laura Howe (10)
Green Park Combined School

I Should Like To . . .

I should like to paint the crunch of the autumn leaves
The attraction of the magnet
I should like to hear the vapour through the chimney
The scudding of the clouds
I would like to feel the words in a book
The growth of nature
I would like to taste the warmth of the sun
The whirling of the tornado
I should like to smell the cheerfulness of the bride
The melancholy widow
I should like to see the creaking of the step
The crisped, fresh air.

Juliet Aldridge (11)
Green Park Combined School

A Goldfish And A Conker Tree

Not a fair comparison really:
Fish don't stand around in lonely parks,
swaying in the cool breeze,
sprouting leaves. They also don't
have eager children climbing up them.

But conker trees don't swim calmly
around in small bowls, blowing bubbles,
and they are not made into credit cards.

I'd rather be a tree,
but a goldfish is easier.

Nicholas Onan-Read & Lee Cahill (11)
Green Park Combined School

The Hunter

The ultimate hunter majestically prowls over barren grassland.
Her soft golden fur is disturbed by an occasional passing breeze.
Scorching rays create a blinding light,
But still she moves on.
Suddenly she halts.
Concealed by the Savannah,
Watchful eyes gaze intently as she waits for her prey.
She slinks behind sharp rocks,
Lying in wait.
Camouflaged.
A deer, unaware of the presence of its hunter settles to graze.
She pounces.
Her prey lies dead,
Lifeless.
Still.

Alison Ings (11)
Green Park Combined School

Parrot

Moving gracefully,
She soars,
High above the Earth,
Brightly coloured feathers catch sun's rays,
She hovers,
She slowly descends to her nest,
Her young squawking happily,
As she supplies them with
Much welcomed fruit and nuts.

Laura Bottoms (11)
Green Park Combined School

STRIPED STALKER

As the blazing fireball sets
Over the horizon
The mother leaves her cubs
And the hunt begins she spies a lonely buffalo
Creeping forward, her eyes
Concentrate on the herd.
The dry bush provides perfect camouflage.
Suddenly the herd halts, knowing a
Predator is near.
A chase begins
In one pounce
The victim lies dead,
Lifeless
Still
Her young will not need to be fed for days.

Joanne Jenkins (11)
Green Park Combined School

SNOW LEOPARD

Her glaring eyes watch,
As she awaits the moment,
Waiting,
She goes for the kill,
Pounces on her unaware victim,
As she bites the neck of her prey,
Her white fur coat gleams in the sun,
She proudly picks up her meal,
And drags it back to her territory.

Becky Loake (11)
Green Park Combined School

CAT

A mouse eater
A feline friend
A fur washer
A fast runner
A flea finder
A ferocious fighter
A vicious biter.

David Brooks (10)
Green Park Combined School

I SHOULD LIKE TO . . .

I should like to paint the whirling wind
in the whistling trees.
I should like to hear the happiness travelling
through people.
I should like to feel friendship's hand.
I should like to see fresh air brushing across my face.
I should like to smell the smell of laughter.

Sarah (10) & Kayleigh Hurley (11)
Green Park Combined School

GOLD

The immense pile of dazzling.
A blinding experience of life.
A satisfying wake-up call.
The elaborate light beaming down
on fragile faces.
The most amazing sight of all.

James Chaplin (10)
Green Park Combined School

GRASSHOPPER

Sun's rays surreptitiously sink behind distant hills,
bathing the fields in a gentle glow.
The first guest arrives,
his wiry body dressed from
head to toe in a dinner suit of emerald.
He takes his place on centre stage
and begins to mesmerise his audience with a
mystical tune.
As he plays the tune changes a little,
the speechless audience leaps into a rhythmic dance.
Changing from one partner to another.
While the secretive violinist
plays
his melancholy lullaby.

Nicholas Webb (11)
Green Park Combined School

WHEN I THINK OF HORSES

When I think of horses
I hear
Them running wild and free forcing their
Powerful hooves on the hard firm ground.
I hear them smashing the turf when they gallop by.
Kicking it behind them, their shadow racing around,
Like a tiger running to catch its prey.
As it starts to buck, it starts to play with the other horses.
And so at last they all settle down for the end of the day.

Libby Gray (11)
Green Park Combined School

GRACEFUL MOVER

Sun sets over the bush,
Now little light is seen.
Unsuspecting prey graze peacefully,
Unaware that their end is near.
Stripes, like an angry night sky,
Lie scattered over the glossy coat,
Ensuring camouflage.
The herd halts,
The predator crouches, slowly edging
Forward,
Eyeing its prey.
Then it pounces.
Its victim lies silent and still.

Laura Kirkland (11)
Green Park Combined School

STAGBEETLE

Hidden in the dark, damp corner of the garden
Munching little bugs.
Bright red eyes shining
Black, hard armour protecting it.
Hard, antler-like jaws
Searching for food.
Laying on my hairy front
Walking on my hairy legs.
My spotted head glistening in the light
My shining small, smooth back.

Steven Moseley (10)
Green Park Combined School

THE FIGURE

On the first day
I saw a small boy
Playing in the snow
With his mother watching
She was sitting
On the park bench
Reading her book.

On the second day
A white figure stood tall
Faceless and alone
Placed in the middle
Of the local park
Until the young boy
Appeared with his friends.

On the third day
The figure was complete
With a human likeness
Noticed by all children
Playing on the cold winter's day
Wrapped up in warm winter clothes
Playing together trying to keep warm.

On the fourth day
The sun was blazing
And the figure was slowly
Melting away into liquid
Shrinking more minute by minute
Getting smaller and smaller.

Today
The children ran through the
Remaining lumps of snow
Left behind from the cold
Icy figure - the snowman.

Debbie McCaffrey & Joanne Cahill (12)
Green Park Combined School

A HAIRY CREATURE

It camouflages itself in long grass,
It disguises itself in dark parts.
Petrified people shiver in fright
It will scare you in the bathroom at night.
It is long hairy creepy too
Its habitat is quite near you.
So run if you see one
You will be nervous as a mouse.
Its pointy little fangs can kill you just like that.

David Murray (10)
Green Park Combined School

ARACHNID

I lie in wait my trap is prepared,
My sombre body glistens,
Almost like oiled leather,
I float suspended from interminable rope,
Waiting,
Watching,
I climb towards my fragile delicate web,
Anticipating your delightful body.

Mohsin Hashmi (11)
Green Park Combined School

SILENT YET DEADLY

Balancing along brick walls,
He prowls,
Creeping slyly towards unsuspecting prey,
Silently slinking,
One paw after the other,
Moving closer,
He pounces,
As quick as lightning.

The victim is caught,
Is it dead or alive?
He delights in the new game,
Tossing and patting the creature about,
Before swaggering back along the wall.

Rebecca Sharman (11)
Green Park Combined School

THE KILLER

Nearer it came
Grinning like a Cheshire cat
I lay helpless, trapped in a silken straight jacket
Walking, stalking, dancing, climbing, closer, closer, closer
Airborne for only a moment
A creature of the ground attempting to fly
Swinging on a thread of silk
Narrowly missing me
It's only a matter of time.

Joanne Westwood (11)
Green Park Combined School

A Golden Eagle

A slow - glider
A wind - rider
A prey - detector
A mouse - selector
A zooming - jet
An illegal - pet
A fish - tearer
A feather - wearer.

Murray Forrest (10)
Green Park Combined School

Elephant

Gradually moving across the desolate landscape,
Searching for succulent leaves.
In the distance he spies an oasis
He quickens his pace to reach it before the others.
He reaches for the luscious leaves in the canopy above.
He lowers them to his waiting mouth.

Jason Peters (10)
Green Park Combined School

Scorpion

I lie in wait
Buried beneath hot sand
My tail carries my most deadly weapon
A paralysing sting
My next victim approaches
I scuttle forwards
Paralysing my prey with my electrifying arrow.

James Hunt (10)
Green Park Combined School

I Should Like To . . .

I should like to paint the ring of a rusty bell,
The sadness of a lonely cub.
I should like to hear the ripples on the fresh water,
The happiness of the golden sun.
I should like to hold the sweet sound of
a singing bird,
The sparkle of the dazzling stars.
I should like to taste the summer flowers,
The clouds spreading across the sky.
I should like to smell the feathers of a peacock,
The stripes of a tiger.
I should like to see the heat of a burning candle,
The coldness of the wind.

Samantha Bates & Emma Barklamb (10)
Green Park Combined School

Tortoise

His wrinkled, lengthy neck stretches
from his hard brown shell,
His prehistoric steady walk is inactive,
His blunt, stubby tail propels behind him
While his sturdy, scaly legs try to make
an exertion
He stops suddenly and sees a striking bunch
of leaves full of essence and greenness.
Slowly his wrinkled neck returns inside his
hard brown shell.

Emma Barklamb (11)
Green Park Combined School

THE EYE

A constant blinker
  A shiny ball
    A stare looker
  A glass circle
A peepy hole
  A coloured dot
    A glimpsing star
  A silent stalker.

Gemma Rainey (10)
Green Park Combined School

SILVER

The glistening light of the moon shines through the windows,
The glimmer of the stars sparkle through the night.
Fishes swimming in the pond,
As gleaming cars go into their drives,
People walk to the shop in the dazzling snow.
As people spend their twinkling coins,
A woman walks past in some shiny jewellery.

Chris Kendall (11)
Green Park Combined School

GOLD

Summer sunset,
Key to a heart,
Warm-hearted glow from an opening door,
A glint of light shines onto the pale windows,
The opening of a new season.

Niki Tibble (11)
Green Park Combined School

TREE HUNTER

I slip on my fur coat and swing
Tree to tree
Day to night
Autumn to winter.
I scour the treetops for delightful fruits and berries
And swing
Tree to tree,
Day to night,
Autumn to winter.
Acrobatic like, I pivot and turn, effortlessly swinging
From branch to branch
Enjoying the applause and admiration.

Michelle Cole (10)
Green Park Combined School

IMPOSSIBLE POEM

I should like to paint the hum of the humming bird,
The furthest star from Earth,
I should like to taste the gleam of the moon,
The summer breeze,
I should like to hear the universe singing,
The ice-cream melting,
I should like to see the voices of people,
The big bang exploding.

Kelly Redman & Laura Bottoms (11)
Green Park Combined School

HUNTER

The terrifying hunter lies in wait,
until the time is right,
He pounces.
Airborne for no more than a few seconds,
The innocent victim is forced through
His coiling body,
Black scales caress smooth skin like an overcoat,
His powerful body slips away surreptitiously
Ready to kill his next victim.

Shane Shah (10)
Green Park Combined School

I SHOULD LIKE TO . . .

I should like to paint unknown creatures in the
depths of the ocean,
The moon's reflection on the water's surface,
I should like to understand the call of the whale,
The sound of fish swimming
The forgotten mystery of the Titanic
I would like to swim with dolphins and glide
effortlessly through the water,
I should like to touch the crest of a wave,
And the constant ebb and flow of the changing tide.

Gemma Fretwell (11)
Green Park Combined School

FIVE HOURS AT A CONCERT

In the first hour,
The tickets are rustling,
People are grabbing,
The front row seats,
And they sit in silence.

In the second hour,
The crowd whispers,
As the group rushes in,
The band says hello as they pick up their instruments.

In the third hour,
The silence turns to screaming,
As the band begins to sing,
The screaming echoes around the room.

In the fourth hour,
The stage is covered in,
Teddy bears and roses,
Names of the people in the band,
Are being screamed out,
So loudly.

In the fifth hour,
They sing their final song,
The crowd goes wild as they leave
The stage.

The room is now so very empty.

Kimberley Harvey (11)
Green Park Combined School

NIGHT HUNTER

Silently he glides upwards
Leaving the antiquated barn behind
Only the shimmering light from the moon
Can guide him on his way

Hovering like a ghost high above the fields
He watches
And listens
Patiently waiting for a sudden movement
He descends and swoops, sharp claws outstretched
Ready to devour his prey.

Katie Nelson (10)
Green Park Combined School

SPIDER

A fly eater,
A small creature,
A good knitter,
A quick spinner,
An eight-legged frightener,
An insect fighter,
A clever catcher,
A body snatcher.

Oliver Gordon (10)
Green Park Combined School

THE SHIP OF DREAMS

I should like to paint the ship of dreams
That sank beneath the ocean.
I should like to hear the lifeless screams.
The sound of the moaning deck splitting in two.
The mystery of the Titanic lays unknown.
I should like to touch the heart of the ocean
And the collection of Rose's precious paintings.

Lily Martin (11)
Green Park Combined School

BROWNIE

Brownie is a teddy bear, he likes to play tennis
and Brownie also has a little friend called Dennis.
Brownie is a teddy bear, he looks very cute.
Brownie also knows a bear who likes to play the flute.
Brownie is a teddy bear, he has two dogs.
He takes them for walks and they sometimes see hedgehogs.

Chrissy Bunyan (7)
Grenville Combined School

TUDOR BATTLE

I'm going to a battle, the battle is at sea.
But what I can't quite understand is why they chose me.
The smells are terrible and the bread they make, why it's enough to give anyone a headache!
Beacons blaze, cannons fire.
It's the worst thing my heart could desire.
Sorry times out, got to get in.
The battle is about to begin!
Yuk, yuk what a horrible smell, I really don't feel very well.
Aye aye Captain, I'll be up there soon, up in the crow's nest.
Boom, boom, boom!
Arrgh! My ears are ablaze.
That cannon gave me quite a daze.
Uh-oh, here it comes, a great explosion from some guns.
Oh dear, poor old me.
My fate shall be at the bottom of the sea.
For that cannon has pierced our boat.
Now it shall not ever again float.

      Glug . . .
           glug . . .
                glug . . .

Claire Bunyan (9)
Grenville Combined School

CONDUCTORS

Conductors always get me,
Into quite a muddled state,
Beating and waving their arms about
As if they were part of a debate.

Nicole Abdul (10)
High March School

Clouds

See the clouds,
Their light spirit
Moving swiftly 'cross the sky,
They are not loud
But move gently overhead.

The large cumulus
The soft cirrus
And all the other types,
They look like dragons, castles,
And even knights!

And then there's the rain clouds,
So loud, so angry!
They pour down with rain and thunder,
But give life to all the plants below.

I lay and watch these beautiful things,
They look so peaceful across the blue summer sky,
So free, so merry, such a pleasure to me.

Jennifer Nicolaison (9)
High March School

Puppies

Puppies are cute and cuddly too,
They'll chew on anything, even a shoe,
Puppies leap, run and prance,
They skip and hop and love to dance,
Puppies, puppies, they're so sweet!
With little paws and tiny feet.
And now this poem has to end,
Saying 'Goodbye' to our little friend.

Natasha Cleland (11)
High March School

THE SHELL

Some say it's like a fairy's home,
Some say it's a part of an ice-cream cone.

Some say it's a water slide,
Some say it's a pasta that's dried.

Most say it's a stone from hell,
But I think it's a simple shell.

Alexandra Wain (11)
High March School

PIGS DO NOT FLY

Pigs do not fly
It is impossible to do,
Pigs do not fly
Like a bit of pie in the sky,
Even if the pig had the flu,
Even if the mad ghost said, 'Boo!'
Pigs do not fly.

Emma Hopkins (10)
High March School

MY SHELL

I thought it looked like a summer hat
That I would wear in Barbados,
I thought it looked like a ski slope
Which I would see in France.
I turned it upside down
And thought it looked like a winter egg,
All coated with mist and frost.

Lauren Carter (9)
High March School

TINKER THE KITTEN

Jet black cats you can't see at night,
Apart from their tiny shiny eyes.
Her eyes are green,
Her paws are small.
And she's soft and cuddly like a
Little black ball.
She chases the flies, and jumps
At the bees.
But most of the time she jumps like the fleas.

Charlotte Matthews (9)
High March School

SUNSET

Night is coming,
Drums are drumming,
Long gone in the morning,
Longer gone the dawning,
The sky is orange and red,
Small children are beginning to go to bed,
For it is time to leave the day behind,
It's time to say 'Goodnight,'
So let the moon shine down on you,
With all its happy light!

Clare Conway (11)
High March School

SPRING

Little daisies have bloomed by my pond,
Daffodils are swaying bright and blonde,
Blossom is on my favourite tree,
It's springtime again for you and me!

Tulips have grown by my swing,
Dandelions are dancing and singing,
Snowdrops are showing their bright white hair,
It's spring in my garden everywhere!

Laura Young (8)
High March School

SNOWFLAKES

S hivering cold, wintry day,
N obody is outside in the freezing chill,
O ver the hills it is as white as icing on a cake,
W inter cold, frosty day.
F lakes flutter to the ground,
L akes are slippery as an ice rink,
A nimals hibernating from the winter cold,
K ingfishers surviving in the trees,
E veryone is warm in their homes,
S omeone's snowman is standing in trousers.

Ravneek Cheema (9)
High March School

BUTTERFLY

Butterfly, butterfly, how you flutter and fly,
Looking so beautiful in the sky.
Butterfly, butterfly, your lovely colours,
So much brighter than all the others.
Butterfly, butterfly, when you're about,
All the children shriek and shout.
Butterfly, butterfly, how you flutter and fly,
When you die, we all cry.

Sara Salehian (8)
High March School

Jack Frost

J ack Frost nibbles your toes,
A nimals hibernate in their warm beds,
C otton wool falls from the sky,
K ing Winter rules the land.

F ire inside lovely and warm,
R osy red robin's breast,
O ak trees covered in snow,
S kating across the icy lake,
T ingling toes from the freezing cold.

Rebecca Duncan (8)
High March School

Snow And Frost

S ilhouette of a mystery man on the lawn so bright,
N o footprints are left from our snowman.
O n every leaf and branch they seem to whisper to me.
W hen the feathery frosts come by, spreading only by night.

A robin whistles his lonely tune,
N ever ceasing to blow this way and that.
D are I think who it might be?

F rosting everything in sight,
R ound the garden at black of night,
O ver hill, and tree and vale
S inging like a nightingale,
T he impish Jack Frost is here again.

Emma Horn (9)
High March School

SHELL

What is this strange form,
All shiny white?
Mother of pearl with a gentle touch of pale brown.

Do I see stripes of blue, sky blue,
In this object deep inside?
I feel in a great storm, roaming and raging while tipping me up at the end.

I see myself falling onto a flock
Of glossy clouds floating past,
Like sheep, running away from my view.

Emily Watson (10)
High March School

A SHELL

A minute hole in the middle
That neither you nor I could get through,
Tiny holes
That rabbits, as small as dust,
Could creep through
To reach the safety
Of the mother of pearl cove,
As shiny as diamonds
When the sun sets,
Coral, as sharp as knives
Waiting to pounce on you,
All these treasures are in my shell.

Lucy Blake (9)
High March School

THE MAGICAL GLASS

It has a face just like a human
Feeling pale because of flu,
Its handle ears would match a mouse,
Its legs would suit a table.
It reminds me of a turtle
Wandering around the lonely beach,
Waiting patiently for the moment
When the tide rushes in.
The hands move around the face
Like three squirrels playing chase,
The handle is a rainbow
Formed between two puffy clouds,
At the centre we hear bees
Buzzing away in their hive,
Their honey pouring over the edges,
Forming a golden coat,
Twelve ladies lie sunbathing,
Waiting to get a tan,
In all, this is a magical glass,
Taking you back to the world's beginning,
Ticking away till the end of time,
A dark well which never ends.

Lisa Rust (11)
High March School

SNOW

S parkling snowflakes silently float down to earth,
N umb hands roll up snowballs and hurl them everywhere,
O n wooden sledges people race down slippery hills,
W inds of all speeds race all around the town.

Lizzie Heeley (8)
High March School

Bonfires

Bonfires glow red and gold
Like the sun in Africa
At its highest point.

Bonfires give off colour and warmth
Making everyone rosy cheeked
And cosy.

Bonfires crackle and spit
Sending sparks flying,
Making Guy Fawkes start dying.

In other words:
Bonfires are my favourite things!

Emily Green (9)
High March School

THE SHELL

Small, alone, but fascinating,
It sits in the palm of my hand.
If, with others, it's dull and uninteresting
When alone, it's the jewel of the land.

A pearl of the sea it may be,
On a hill with lots of ropes
Descending down the sloping plain
On the antlers of antelopes.

Once an animal lives in this
A fine home it must be,
To live in a luxury of splendour
In the pearl or the jewel of the sea!

Lottie Greenhow (10)
High March School

My Box

Towering high above my desk
I proudly present to you,
My box with sea shells fastened
I think it's lovely, don't you?

The summit swerves with leopard spots
Above the rest of the shells,
A purple cave with cobwebs
Below the summit lies.

That cobweb is very surprising,
Like a curtain plain,
And on the other side I see
A sea shell with a yellow stain.

The little shells on here are scattered
In many different ways,
Spotted, plain or simple
I love them all the same.

Veronika Riedl (10)
High March School

What Is Special About November?

Up, up, up
Into a black, black sky.
Red, orange, yellow
Burning a home-made guy.

Sparkle, sparkle, sparkle
Go the children's eyes,
As rockets and fountains
Begin to rise.

Fun, fun, fun
It is so much fun!
Dazzling and deafening
For everyone.

Nothing to see, see, see,
Nothing to hear, hear, hear.
Everybody's gone home,
But they'll be back next year!

Louise Bralsford (9)
High March School

HORSES AND PONIES

Horses and ponies gallop around
Hear their hooves upon the ground,
Marmalade, strawberry and flash of grey
Welcome the morn of a brand new day.

Pinks and blues of the morning sky
Dew like teardrops on grasses high,
They hear the buzzing of busy bees
And see black silhouettes of trees.

After their precious moments of play
Each one is caught and lead away,
There in the stable they stand so still
Before being ridden over the hill.

Back at the stable, weary and tired
But happy they've been so much admired,
Fast asleep in stable warm
Safe from wind and hail and storm.

Katy Bell (8)
High March School

SNOWFLAKES

S nowflakes gently fall from the sky,
N ever do they fail to make a blanket of snow,
O n they go, never ceasing just fall, fall, fall,
W hite and delicate,
F luttering gently down.
L ook at them descending from the sky,
A mbling along their route,
K ids lick them as they fall,
E very one made of lace,
S lowly, they melt as the sun comes out.

Rachel Harris (8)
High March School

JACK FROST

J umping, skipping through the night,
A crobating, flips and turns, in candlelight.
C limbing walls, and setting curses;
K ing of frost and ice.

F lying round your roof tops,
R acing down frozen streams.
O n the pillow of your bed,
S liding up to freeze your head!
T ing-ting the icy fingers of the ice king!

Sarah Ratner (8)
High March School

JACK FROST

Jack Frost, the servant of the ice, comes at night
And blows his frozen breath everywhere,
Coldness comes when his job is done
King of the cold, his power behold.

Frost takes over the world and the world turns white,
Reign he must on a cold winter morning,
Over the mountains you see him come,
Slow is the sun to melt his doing
To see Jack Frost leap over the fields is a privilege indeed.

Louise Hatton (9)
High March School

SNOW

Long icicles grow,
Old puddles are now white,
It is icy cold.

Poor animals die,
All the trees are covered in snow,
Every bit of sun counts.

Buses get stuck in the snow,
Tramps stay in their caravans,
Winter stings every finger and then moves on.

Elizabeth Andrew (9)
High March School

WINTER

Winter wonderland has come again,
Icy rivers to skate on,
Numb fingers all day long,
Tumbling down a mountain on skis,
Early in the morning is time for hot chocolate,
Ripples of snow turn into ice, ice, ice!

Cassie Macleod (8)
High March School

ROBIN

R ed breasted little bird,
O h, what a lovely song you sing
B ecause the sun is risen. Yet,
I n my bed I snuggle warm,
N ow I know it is Christmas morn.

Emily Halley (8)
High March School

A WILLOW IN THE WIND

A willow waved in the wind,
Streams slither along slowly,
A dragonfly danced upon the stream,
The stream slithered slowly
To the willow in the wind.

Jane Fuerst (10)
High March School

The Frosty Moon

Silently, snow like talcum powder falls from the sky,
When night comes
Icicles sparkle by the light.

Cosy in my warm bed,
The frosty moon flying in the sky,
I say, 'Goodnight, man in the moon
And sleep well too.'

Amy Duncan (8)
High March School

The Little Grey Mouse

The little grey mouse has a hole for his house
Where he hides away and disappears,
The little grey mouse runs away from cats and mousetraps,
He hurries and scurries in fright,
The little grey mouse finds cheese and some cake
Which he loves so he is really pleased,
The little grey mouse has tiny paws and a long tail,
He is so sweet to see.

Caroline Carter (9)
High March School

Dolphins

Dolphins are the most beautiful creatures,
Their gleaming eyes and unusual features,
They leap and dive, look so alive,
Swim so fast and always last,
For forty years or more.

Sophie Burness (9)
High March School

My Marble

The swirls tangle over each other,
Like a multicoloured ball of wool,
The blue spiral like an ever winding river,
Bridged in yellow and orange,
Like a number eight
Or a long scarf wrapped around
While I float away in space.

Genevieve Watson (9)
High March School

The Silver Horse

The silver horse runs through the trees
Bending in and out with ease.
The light glistens on her shiny back
The field mouse watches from her crack.
The silver horse spreads her wings
And they shimmer and shine like diamond rings.

Lizzie Trott (10)
High March School

A Shell

A dark deep pit,
A massive warm swimming pool,
A gloomy dark cave with a bat inside,
An eagle flying through the shining sun,
A woolly jumper as cosy as can be,
All these are hiding in my shell.

Claira Evans (9)
High March School

Floating Kaleidoscope

Colourful bubbles, glittering shapes
Falling like magic and dancing along.
Golden, turquoise, red and silver,
Green, orange and rich purple.
Looking like a delicious fruit salad
Drifting away in a dream
To where the moon is floating.
An erupting volcano of stars
In a distant land,
Like a treasure chest full of golden crystals
Clear as a stream.
Falling like colourful sea waves,
Crashing against the rocks,
Wonderful shapes, like hearts of love
Shining like diamonds,
Sailing away in space.

Lucie Stangl (9)
High March School

Jack Frost

J umping through bushes,
A cross the green grass,
C ackling in the air,
K ing of all the sprites.

F rozen all around,
R ushing and jumping so fast,
O pening his silver shimmering cloak,
S inging and dancing about,
T oo fast to catch.

Charlotte Rees (8)
High March School

JACK FROST

J umping about like a spring,
A ll around he spreads frost like a sprinkler,
C amouflaged but coming to your house soon,
K icking the freezing crystals to spread them.

F rozen hard as the icy ground,
R acing around to complete it by the morning,
O n the garden he dances as lively as a grasshopper,
S inging a merry tune as sweet as a bird song,
T urning round and round like a wheel.

Claire Field (9)
High March School

I WAS THE BEST

The ball was bouncing off the bat
And I was running like a cat,
I couldn't really run fast
So the ball went whizzing straight past,
But then someone hit the ball
And I caught it,
All the people were shouting -
Yes, yes, I was the best.

Lauren Fitzpatrick (10)
High March School

SNOW ALERT!

Shivering I went out to the damp garden,
Nearby on the trees icicles hung,
Over by the pond snowflakes fluttered down
Whispering, just begun.

Snowballs crunch under my feet,
Tedious chilblains grow,
Over the hill I go
Reaching out to the top,
My journey will soon be done.

Clare Thomas (8)
High March School

My Marble

It is smooth and shiny
Like your hand in some water,
I can see blue and white crystals
In a dark black cave,
The sea with sunlight
Shining down on it at dawn,
The dolphins are swimming happily
And waves are splashing and crashing
On top of other glistening waves.

Carolyn Eaton (10)
High March School

Autumn

Autumn is here
As golden leaves drift to the ground,
Autumn is here.
As you rake them up, aim to clear,
Prancing around like a young hound
As if they don't want to be found,
Autumn is here.

Sarah Filler (11)
High March School

Rain

It came like tears,
Falling down from the snowy clouds,
It came like tears,
But then it touched the ground and died,
And thousands more came to touch earth,
Like they were going to their death,
It came like tears.

Nicola Jones (10)
High March School

Fireworks

Sparklers sizzling and crackling on the burnt stick,
Catherine wheels swirling, the colours a blur on the metal pole,
Rockets zooming into the dark blue sky,
Golden rain shooting up
And floating down in shiny trails of stars,
All fireworks are pretty on November the fifth.

Gemma Bradshaw (9)
High March School

Lizards

I like my lizards very much,
When they hunt and play,
They wave their tails round and round,
Then jump on their prey,
The crickets try to avoid the snapping jaws,
When they come their way,
But the lizards are too fast for them,
They don't always miss the prey!

Jane Ashby (11)
High Wycombe CE Combined School

THE BURGLARS

'Look! There it is!' he whispered in my ear,
'Speak a bit louder, I really can't hear!'
'Over there, behind the trees at the foot of the hill,
Next to the lamppost, in front of the mill.'
'Where? I can't see it, you're taller than me,
It's not fair! How come I was born short and podgy?'
'Oh just shut up and go, before it's too late!'
'I can't. I need the toilet, don't think I can wait!'

      'Are we nearly there yet? I've blisters on my blisters!'
      'Don't be such a wimp; you're even worse than my sisters.
      About two more yards, and we're outside the door,
      Now stop complaining, you're being a bore!'

'We're inside the house, and it's dark in here,
What if a spider scuttles right by my ear?
I'm supposed to keep watch, in case someone comes,
But I'm scared of the dark; (don't tell my mum!)'

      'Oh no! What's that noise? I heard something, I'm sure.
      This is it! It's the end! I'll be in jail ever more!
      If he doesn't come soon, I'll cry, I will!
      Don't think I won't, I've just left school.
      That's it, I'm going, and not coming back.
      He for once can take the rap.'

'I'm outside the door, shutting it, *smack!*
Walking down the path, and not looking back.'

Katy Thompsett (12)
High Wycombe CE Combined School

TELETUBBIES

There are four Teletubbies,
Each one of them is cute,
Laa-Laa is the yellow one,
But they all have little boots.
There are four Teletubbies,
They can't talk very much,
Po is the little red one,
And the rabbits, they are Dutch.
There are four Teletubbies,
They like to eat strange food,
The other ones are boys,
But none of them are rude.
There are four Teletubbies,
It's time to go to bed,
Read a bedtime story,
And then lay down your head.

Anna Lancaster (11)
High Wycombe CE Combined School

SPAGHETTI LETTERS IN BAKED BEANS

When I'm feeling lonely,
And I'm going to extremes,
I feel like spaghetti,
In a sea of baked beans.

I feel like I'm different,
Think other people better,
But then I think that they're baked beans,
And I'm spaghetti letters!

Spaghetti letters spell your name,
Baked beans slide off your fork,
Spaghetti letters speak for themselves,
But baked beans seldom talk.

It's not that I don't like baked beans,
I think they're pretty cool,
But though deep down we're all the same,
I'm an individual!

Elizabeth Hoyle (12)
High Wycombe CE Combined School

ST VINCENT BORN

Pebbly beaches, coconut trees,
Sweet scents of George Town,
Sugar apples, mango fruits, sugar cane
And Mauby bark
A small town, left at less than one
Kept by secrets in my mind,
They were planted by nan,
By lovely sounds,
Rumbling volcanoes
Tickling my brain
Almalloching the ocean's roar
And I am St Vincent
Bound to go.

Aaron Henry (12)
High Wycombe CE Combined School

MY ALIEN FRIEND

My alien friend lives in outer space,
My alien friend is a completely different race.
My alien friend has green and blue toes,
My alien friend has an oblong nose.
My alien friend is very ornate,
My alien friend is quite a mate.
My alien friend is as big as a bear,
Yet my alien friend is as quick as a hare.
My alien friend has a re-arranged face,
My alien friend has hair as fine as lace.
As my relationship with my alien began to uncurl,
I found that my alien is out of this world.

Tom Davies (11)
High Wycombe CE Combined School

ANIMALS IN AUTUMN

Animals are as bright as the sun.
Animals are as dark as the moon.
Squirrels are collecting nuts as fast as can be.
Badgers are digging burrows deep underground.
Some animals are as fast as the wind.
Some animals are as slow as the leaves.
Some burrows are messy and gloomy.
Some burrows are very clean.
Most animals start to hibernate
Before the winter comes.
Some animals sleep like logs.
Others only sleep lightly.

Sophie Binks (9)
Holy Trinity CE County Middle School

MY HAIKU POEM

It is very warm
Look at that boiling bright sun
Yes now it's raining.

It is very cold
Look at that frost in the sky
Look at the black cloud.

Luke Hudson (9)
Holy Trinity CE County Middle School

MY AUTUMN POEM

In the autumn it's as cold as ice,
And the leaves are as small as mice.
The sun is bright as can be,
My breath is steamy.
The conkers fall off the trees,
And the cold makes me sneeze.
The rain is as wet as water,
It makes the mud look like chocolate.

Jack Guttery (9)
Holy Trinity CE County Middle School

HAIKU POETRY

The path is soaking,
Because of the drumming rain,
I am getting wet.

Hazel Inniss (9)
Holy Trinity CE County Middle School

A Windy Day

Winter is cold.
The leaves crunch up.
The winter gets colder.
Then the grass freezes up.
I see everyone shivering.
In a coat.

Sam Turner (8)
Holy Trinity CE County Middle School

One Snowy Day

The snow is cold, the snow is freezing
on this snowy day.
The wind is breezy, it makes me sneezy
on this snowy day.
The snow is everywhere, the children are playing
on this snowy day.
The mist is rising, the rain is pouring
on this snowy day.

Luke Godfrey (8)
Holy Trinity CE County Middle School

Haiku Poetry

Everything is white.
My window-pane has frozen.
It's very cold out.

Jade Knowlden (9)
Holy Trinity CE County Middle School

The Cold And Frosty Winter's Morning

When it's a frosty morning.
Frost on the window.
Frost on the door.
Frost on the doorbell.
Frost on the wall.

When it's a frosty morning.
No one is outside because it is cold.
They stay inside so they don't get cold.
If you went outside you would probably freeze.
The winter's so cold you wouldn't believe.

Christian Foy (8)
Holy Trinity CE County Middle School

My Autumn Poem

Golden leaves fall off the trees
Autumn's here again.
As we walk we scrunch and
Crunch
Winter's almost here.
All the leaves have fallen off the trees
Golden, brown, yellow too
The whole ground is covered in leaves
Birds begin to fly away
Far away from the cold.

Kelly Weston (8)
Holy Trinity CE County Middle School

WINTER

The snow is thick.
The house roofs are covering in snow.
We wear thick clothes outside.
December has come.
We make a snowman in the garden.
The snowman has eight buttons, a hat,
A scarf, and carrot for his nose.
December has come.
Now it's time to go to bed.
The sky is black.
There is no moon.
December has come.
In the morning there is more snow.
I make my snowman bigger by adding more snow.
December has come.

Phillip Bryant (9)
Holy Trinity CE County Middle School

WINTER IS COMING

Misty fog all around
Winter's coming.
Gloomy snow falling down
Winter's coming.
Ice crunching, rain falling
Winter's coming.
Trees' leaves falling down
Winter's coming.

Francesca Randall (8)
Holy Trinity CE County Middle School

RAINDROPS IN WINTER

When rain falls you hear a splash.
Winter raindrops are here.
People jump in puddles.
Winter raindrops are here.
Raindrops are made by clouds.
Winter raindrops are here.
You stay indoors when rain drops.
Winter raindrops are here.
People wrap up warm.
Winter raindrops are here.
When you walk around rain goes in your face.
Winter raindrops are here.

Faye Devereux (9)
Holy Trinity CE County Middle School

HAIKU POETRY

The wind is howling
The clouds are black in the sky
The trees are swaying.

Kayleigh Melling (9)
Holy Trinity CE County Middle School

LEAVES

Golden leaves like the sun.
Falling like the rain.
Crunching on my feet.
Fun like playing.
It must be autumn.

Amy Foskett (8)
Holy Trinity CE County Middle School

POTION, LOTION

In the deep blue ocean,
a multicoloured fishy
saw a potion.
He gulped it down ever
so quick that he was
nearly sick.

He went to bed that
night feeling all right.
When he woke up in
the morning he was
crimson red, so he thought
I'm going to stay in bed.

In a few hours he found
he had magical powers
and he zapped himself
in the head.
In a few years this
fishy called Ted knew
just what to do.
He put on shows for
all of his friends and
wore a frilly, pink tutu.

Leanne Oxlade (11)
Lent Rise School

THE UNDERWATER MELODY

Down in the angry deep I go searching
Searching for the underwater melody
'Tis a wonderful and magical experience
That you would really wish to see.

Oysters open and shutting just like the sound of cymbals
Fishes tap on turtles' bellies just like the bashing of drums
The dolphins' voices echo through the sea
Mermaids pluck on lobsters' whiskers like the sound of harps
Whales hit their tails on the sea
Seaweed swayed and brushed against the rocks just like the
plucking of guitars
Crabs sang gentle harmonies whilst clapping their claws
Seals dancing with each other on the rocks
Flatfish swim around so fast giving it the feeling
The sun shines through the sea shining on the sand floor!
Then there's me left to be the audience, really I enjoyed it.

It's almost finished
The animals are settled, almost asleep
I am so very tired after a magical experience
I promise I will go again
To visit all my friends
Also sit listen and watch the underwater melody
And never get bored
So see you tomorrow.

Zoe Austin (11)
Lent Rise School

MY CAT MILLIE

My cat Millie is a lovely little cat
A fluffy cat
A ginger cat
My cat Millie is a hungry little cat
A greedy cat
A lapping cat
My cat Millie is a wild little cat
A pouncing cat
A prowling cat
My cat Millie is a gentle little cat
A purring cat
A cuddly cat
My cat Millie is a sleeping little cat
A stretching cat
A yawning cat
My cat Millie is a naughty little cat
A scratching cat
A playful cat
My cat Millie is a loving little cat
A cute cat
And I'm her lucky owner.

Lauren Austin (8)
Lent Rise School

EGYPT

Egypt is where the pharaohs rest,
Gold and silver in their chest,
Years ago where they lay to rest,
People today still look in wonder,
Towards the pyramids that gods lay under.

Michael Burfoot (11)
Lent Rise School

A May Day

The wind was blowing,
the trees were growing.
The boys would play
in lovely May.
The grass was bright green
the flowers could be seen.
Did you know the river
would flow, nearby the grass
where you would pass,
the colourful flowers?
During the day the sun
shone bright.
As it faded away then came night.
As you looked in the sky
and saw the stars.
Someone said one could be Mars.
I looked up and saw the Milky Way.
That was the end of a
perfect May day.

Jack Groves (10)
Lent Rise School

What Shall I Do Today?

Yesterday I sat all day,
The day before I ran,
But today I'm going to twist and turn everywhere I can,
Over yellow mountains and across the big wide sea,
Then back in my garden where everyone can
See me.

Katie Bisgrove (10)
Lent Rise School

THE CUP FINAL

It was a sunny afternoon in the month of May
When two football teams came to play,
One in red, the other in blue,
One goal in mind to win it through.
The blue team kicked off at such a pace that the next thing,
They knew, the blue team had scored, what a disgrace.
The crowd shouted hip, hip, hooray.
The red team were in disgrace.
They knew they had to set the pace.
The fight back was hard, the fight back was long,
But through sustained pressure they had equalised.
One all at extra time.
The game in balance with not much to go,
Who would win, who would lose, the supporters did not know.
Then in that last moment of the game,
The reds had struck again!
So there they had it, it was two-one,
The trophy was theirs!

Tommy Clifford (9)
Lent Rise School

A DAY BY THE SEA

I spend the day by the sea,
With seagulls flying over me,
The water rippling on the sand,
Makes me think it's rather grand,
Oh look there's a band playing music
While people stand and tap their feet,
On the cobbles that make up the street.

Christopher David Argrave (10)
Lent Rise School

SPRING

Bright yellow daffodils with orange trumpets,
Pale white snowdrops covering the hills like a blanket,
Tiny mauve and yellow crocus push through the ground,
Pink and white blossoms look like birds have sprinkled confetti
                                                            all around.

Woolly lambs in the meadow bleat for food,
Brown rabbits hop to their burrows,
Girls and boys skipping with delight down the country lane,
They are collecting tadpoles from the pond once again,
These are all the things that remind me of spring,
And of nature which is a wonderful thing.

Emma Anderton (8)
Lent Rise School

STRANGER, STRANGER!

I was in the park one day
A man came over and said did I want to play?
I thought to myself what do I say?
But I said nothing and ran away.
I told my mum.
She said she would come
To the park because it was getting dark.
We went to the police
Who said I did well.
They said *you always must tell.*

Nicholas Kennedy (9)
Lent Rise School

DREAMS

Dreams are sometimes very strange, of people playing silly games.
People running round and round or things bouncing up and down.
Monsters living in your tummy or Dracula trying to eat up
your mummy!
Trapped inside a spooky house running after a dirty mouse!
Or...
Sheep prancing in the field with cows and chicks and daffodils.
A land full of chocolate swirls or people with dainty toes.
Having a picnic on the beach having something nice to eat.
Going somewhere really nice or playing a game with very clean mice.
People jumping everywhere or people with lovely hair, hugging a
very big bear...
Or maybe...
Laying comfortably in your bed, with nothing at all in your head!

Gemma Campbell (11)
Lent Rise School

SPACE

Rockets flying into space
Just look upon that person's face
Orbiting the Earth at the same pace.

Dancing with the stars and wondering
Is there life on Mars?
One thing for sure there aren't any cars.

Back to earth from the space station
The astronaut is a hero of the nation
Searching planets to find their creation.

Daniel Russell (10)
Lent Rise School

CHELSEA, CHELSEA

Chelsea, Chelsea are the best,
They can beat all the rest.
The players come from far and wide,
This makes up a competitive side.
Vialli, Zola, Wise and Flo,
When they run they really go.
For a goalie who can save the day,
De Goey and Kharine can play.
For penalties you can take your pick
From Petriescu and Lebeouf to take the kick.
Chelsea were in the title race
Until Man Utd stepped up the pace.
In Europe we are doing well
As Tromso and Slovan Bratislava fell.
But I'm a Chelsea supporter through and through,
And all my life I'll follow the blues.

Matthew Fenwick (10)
Lent Rise School

WEATHER

On a cold damp winter's day,
when the wind and rain make it look grey,
you can look out of the window and think of the sun,
and look forward to the summer and having some fun.
When the snow starts to fall and turning to ice,
you can think of your holiday and all that is nice.
When the spring arrives with the light evening nights,
you can think of the winter and the dark evening nights.

Lauren Russell (8)
Lent Rise School

The Lion's Roar

I hate the sound
Of the lion's roar
When horror bites my head.
When lions run through
The jungle banging and
Thumping but is with me.

When ginger eyes are
Gleaming at me but
They're all you see
When he stares at you
Straight in the eye.

He gave a mighty leap
As I awoke from my sleep.

Aidan Williams (11)
Long Crendon C Combined School

The Black Cat

He wonders up and down all day
or lies down in the sun.
I sometimes wonder where he lives
and if he's got a mum.

I wonder if he's got a name?
We could always call him Sam.
My brother takes Sam for a walk
sometimes, he takes him in the pram.

Sarah Martin (10)
Long Crendon C Combined School

FORMULA ONE

The lights are out,
Formula One, racing,
Pit stops all good fun.
Tyres screeching! Crashes!
Blown engines!
All in one day's race.
Speed, speed, only speed.
Skill, skill, only skill.

The first pit stop has come
25 laps through.
What's this? He hasn't stopped!
Oh no what a waste, poor old
Hakkinen.
What has happened?
Why did he do that?
Poor old Hakkinen,
What a shame.

The flag has come,
The race is nearly over,
No more pit stops,
No more fun.

Andrew Cameron (11)
Long Crendon C Combined School

DINOSAUR

What's this in the meadow?
Four big feet,
Does it eat meat?
No, it's a Diplodocus!

What's this in the forest?
Two big claws,
Does it have jaws?
Yes, it's a Megalosaurus!

What's this in the jungle?
Two beady eyes that stare,
Does it have hair?
No, it's a Compsognathus!

What's this on sea shore?
Two whopping great wings,
Not chicken limbs.
You're right, it's a Pteranodon!

What's this in the ocean?
A great long neck,
I like to peck.
Yes, I'm a Plesiosaurus!

What's this in the desert?
A giant carnivore,
King of them all.
You're correct, it's a T Rex!

Kristian Purchase (10)
Long Crendon C Combined School

Cosmic Kid

His face is blue,
His eyes are red,
He sleeps upside down
In a floating bed.
He eats green worms
Alive, not dead
And surprise, surprise
His name is Fred.

Fred likes to swim,
But in air not sea
He races with his friends
And always beats me!
He has a pet rat
With bright orange hair
The only food it eats
Is purple-skinned pear.

His mum and dad
Are kind as kind.
If Fred's naughty
They hardly mind!
His brother and sister
Are both pains in the neck
And if they annoy him,
Fred shouts, 'What the heck!'

So Fred's my mate
'Cos he's never been to school
And everything about him
Is mega, mega cool!

Laura Hastings (11)
Long Crendon C Combined School

STREET CHILD

How would you feel,
All alone in the world?
No one to hug you,
No one to love you.

How would you feel,
Left alone in a war?
Fighting around you,
Hate all around you.

How would you feel
In a bed on the street?
Coldness inside you,
Coldness outside you.

I know how it feels,
I've suffered before.
You may be alright,
In the warmth of your bed,
Someone to love you,
A guarantee to be fed.

But somewhere nearby you,
There's someone like me,
So someone must love them,
Someone must care!

Rosanna Ryan (11)
Long Crendon C Combined School

DT

DT is such fun,
I'm designing some trousers to
Fit over my bum.
The fabric is red, the zip is blue.
I really hope they fit you too.
The top is green,
Yellow and orange,
Purple, brown and blue.
It's multi-coloured, oh what fun.
My mum says it looks like goo.
Stitching, sewing, pinning thumbs,
Working hard, till outfits are done.
Oh what fun.

Amy Smith (11)
Long Crendon C Combined School

The Stalking Cat

Lying low in the grass,
Waiting for a bird to pass.
Suddenly all is still,
For a bird has landed on the window sill.
It is then the cat's chance to pounce,
As the bird hops to the ground with a bounce.
With a crouch, spring and leap,
A cry escapes the bird's beak.
A fly of feathers, flesh and hair,
Has the bird dead in a few minutes spare.
The cat then carries off his prize,
And devours it till sunrise.

Vicki Osborne (11)
Long Crendon C Combined School

Poor Teddy

Dear Nanny
I'm a teddy bear
I'm really confused
A little girl called Annie comes to bed every night
She kisses me, hugs me, she says she loves me
But when she goes to sleep she chucks me out of bed
                                (I can tell you it hurts).
In the morning her mum comes, picks me up,
Puts me in a spinning thing, then she turns it on and it starts to spin,
                                             really fast
(I get really dizzy, it makes a loud noise)
When that's finished I get hung upon the line by my ears (that hurts).
Then the girl comes along takes me off the line, then,
She kisses me, hugs me, she says she loves me.
Then she takes me to the park, she buys an ice-cream for me,
She puts it down my front then blames me for the mess,
We go home for tea and bed.
When she goes to bed she kisses me, hugs me, says she loves me
But when she goes to sleep she chucks me out of bed.
Then everything happens all over again, and again, and again,
                                             and again.
Yours with a bump on the head
                       Bruised teddy

PS Please solve my problem.

Catherine Maxwell (11)
Long Crendon C Combined School

End Of Summer

The end of summer is here
The days are getting shorter
The conkers are becoming ripe
And the days are getting colder

Autumn is here; hip hip hooray
Birds are flying away and away
Conkers drop to the ground
And rabbits jump up and down
Autumn is here; hip hip hooray.

Lauren Michael (11)
Long Crendon C Combined School

ANIMAL ANTICS

The giraffe stretches out his long elegant neck,
his tongue is flung out at the chance of a peck
of green luscious leaves, juicy and flat
while the ant watches in awe, wishing he could do that.

The elephant, they say will never forget,
but he seems to have done, he's broken the Blue Peter set.
His clumpy feet so big and round,
have smashed all the lights and caused such a sound.

The graceful peacock struts about,
he will always speak but never shout.
His bright feathers are a wonderful sight,
will they be extinct soon? They just might.

The ferocious tiger is known for miles around,
to catch his dinner in a single bound.
A little fluffy rabbit washes his face,
he's settled in a home now, this is his place.

Surely no man could ever get rid of these sights,
why would he want to? Animals have rights.
I'll tell you why, for money or fame,
animals are being killed and we are to blame.

Natalie Barnes (11)
Long Crendon C Combined School

Flopsy Poem

Her big white ears flop,
She twitches her nose
Sprinting in the garden
Eating all Mum's flowers.

She has got real running power,
She pulls at the flower
Takes her nearly an hour.

She licks you with her hot tongue,
Suddenly she gives off a smell,
That smells like dung.

She sits on the mat,
Then chases the cat.
She stands on her back,
When you touch her
She gives you a whack.

She really is a lovely rabbit,
But has some horrible habits.

Hannah Young (11)
Long Crendon C Combined School

The Embarrassment

The crowd all cheered,
'Hip hip hooray,
Well done,' they said, in a cheerful way.

As I walked down the alley
In my lovely pink dress,
I stood on my tiptoes and hoped for the best.

I got on the stage
And started to twirl,
My body spinning,
My head in a whirl.

I got off the stage at a rapid pace,
Tripped over my feet,
Fell flat on my face.

Becky Hamment (10)
Long Crendon C Combined School

LET'S PLAY WORMS ON THE COMPUTER

Start the party straight away,
We're gonna play the Worms today.
Kill Howard Wilkinson with a knife,
The Worms are coming,
Run for your life.

Grenades are flying everywhere,
Weapon Drops fall from the air.
Angry captain mops his brow,
Hurls a grenade . . . we're for it now!
What's he up to now? A Mole Bomb!
If he goes on like this my Worms are long gone!

Challenge mode time, no trouble is Spong,
Come on then let's move along.
Give us a break,
James Brown's a fake!
Bobby B consider him dead,
We'll bazooka him in the head!

James Pepper (10)
Long Crendon C Combined School

THE HORSE

She listened carefully for a sound,
A sound so sweet and tender,
The rustling through the autumn leaves,
It must be a complete pretender,
Then she saw his big black eyes,
And glimpsed his silky coat,
And too saw his sparkling ears
And remembered her horse called Doat.

She quickly ran and grabbed him,
His long and furry mane,
She tacked him up completely,
But then it started to rain,
She galloped off very wet,
And said 'Oh, please help me.'
But then her worst of nightmares came,
Ahead she saw a tree,

The tree had fallen to the ground,
She jumped it very quick,
It was the highest she's ever jumped,
And still didn't get a prick.
She galloped back as fast as she could,
And put him in his stable,
She said, 'You are a very good horse,'
And went to the kitchen table.

Alison Penford (10)
Long Crendon C Combined School

The Death

The cold blue room
Not the buzz of a voice.

No TV blaring out loud
No not a sound.

We sit quietly reading books
Nobody looks to see our emotions.

No sound of arguing no not now
Life isn't the same without Great Nan.

Francesca Tonkin (10)
Long Crendon C Combined School

The Barn Owl

Barn owl sleeping quietly
A dormouse wakes
It scuttles along the barn
Floor in pursuit
To a nest of woodlouse,
Owl awakes,
Hears the rustling and scraping.
Ebony eyes flashing crimson
As it swoops down,
Hooked beak and talons picked up
The surprised prey.
Swiftly flying back to the barn.
Swoops again.
The mouse escapes
Disenchanted owl flies back
Into the rafters
To sleep with a satiated stomach.

Katharine Langridge (10)
Maltman's Green School

FRIENDSHIP

Friendship is built by:

F eeling and fondness,
R espect and regard,
I mportance but not impatience,
E steem and encouragement,
N atural negotiation,
D evotion and decency,
S ensitivity but not selfishness,
H appiness and harmony giving an
I rreplaceable
P artnership.

Sarah Carter (1)
Maltman's Green School

FRIENDSHIP

F riends will always be here for you,
R ain, snow, fog or sun.
I n whichever weather, there'll be fun,
E ach of you having a great time.
N ever shall you be alone.
D oing what you want to do,
S inging, dancing or acting,
H e'll/she'll do it too.
I n some sad cases, friendship stops,
P laying ends, fighting begins . . .

Nikki Reale (11)
Maltman's Green School

HELP THE AGED

Every day they care and worry.
Every day more wrinkles come.
Every day they forget what happened the day before.
They need support to be able to do things.
It's not much fun on your own.
Help them unwind.
Make them laugh.
Have fun with them.
'Cause they don't have much
Once they were like us
But age has taken it's toll
Their insides are not working properly
They may have done some horrible or silly things when they
                                                were younger.
They went to night-clubs and had the time of their lives.
They might have had hobbies of all types.
They might have played games in the playground at school
But not any more.

Laura Fedorciow (11)
Maltman's Green School

RAT!

Surreptitiously watching the wood,
Guarding himself against any danger,
Tail starts to move snake-like through the dead leaves
A sleek fur coat shines glossy in the night light,
His head starts to move
There is a squeak,
A soft step across the ground with a crunch from the sticks and leaves,
His whiskers move and his mouth opens,
Crooked ugly discoloured teeth show through.

Elizabeth Jenkins (11)
Maltman's Green School

Help The Aged

Help the aged
They were once just like you
Partying all night with everything to do.

Help the aged
In homes they will be sad and alone
Feeling unwanted, bad, disowned.

Lend a hand
If you can
Help them to shop
Give them hope
Give them a gift
Help them to cope.

They used to have lots to do
But now they just sit
Watching through windows,
Waiting for a visit.

Michaela Hunt (11)
Maltman's Green School

The Weasel

Dusk falls,
The hunt begins
Moving swiftly through the tree
Powerful, aggressive, vicious rodent
Ready for the kill!
This chestnut coloured slender body
Ready to pursue anything that is there
It sees a shrew
It's gone for good!

Sarah Scott (10)
Maltman's Green School

HELP THE AGED

When you look into the old faces,
You can imagine where they have been,
Through World War One and Two,
Through air raids, bombs and fires.
When you look into the old faces
Their old grey eyes turn blue.
If you put them in a home,
All alone
To watch fellow people come and go
You know you'll feel guilty deep inside
But all those choking tears you must hide.
When you look at their old faces,
Their old grey eyes turn blue with the knowledge of life and love.
Some lived through Queen Victoria
Some the birth of Elizabeth and Charles
And HRH Princess Diana
Some won't make the millennium
Others only just.
Go on help the aged
Give them your heart.

Candice Miles (11)
Maltman's Green School

RATS

Dusky black eyes peering into the darkness,
Clear tails swaying in a snake-like manner,
Powerful bodies stock-still in the shadows,
Round beady eyes spying on a small mouse,
His prey.
Thick fur covered pear-shaped body,
Still motionless in the gloomy sewer.

Amy De Marsac (11)
Maltman's Green School

HELP THE AGED

Help the aged they were once like you,
Help the aged they used to smoke and drink like you,
Help the aged they used to party all night like you.

Help the aged they don't want to be alone,
Help the aged they don't want to be put in a home,
Help the aged they don't want to be lonely.

Help the aged they will not live much longer,
Help the aged because you will be like them one day,
Help the aged you will brighten up your life and
                    theirs at the same time.

Help the aged they have such a boring life,
Help the aged they want to go to places,
Help the aged take them to a party.

Help the aged they just sit at home,
Help the aged they want to go outside but
                    they're too frightened.
Help the aged they need some friends.

Help the aged go and make them a cup of tea,
Help the aged even if they're blind or disabled,
Help the aged take them to the shops.

Help the aged make friends with them,
Help the aged take their dogs for a walk,
Help the aged they're not so bad at all.

Jenna Herbert (11)
Maltman's Green School

TIGER

The tiger creeps
among the grass
looking for its
prey
camouflaged by
the stems
it's not seen along
the way.

The feeding deer
is unaware
of danger by its side.
But wait!
Tiger!
Tiger!
Better run and hide.

The deer leaps high
and tries to fly
across the grassy plain
the tiger runs
and makes a lunge
the hunt's not been in vain.

The stunning deer
has been destroyed
as nature has its way
the starving cubs
will eat their fill.
So ends another day.

Anneka Crawley (11)
Maltman's Green School

HELP THE AGED

Help the aged
In their final years
Share their worries
And cure their fears.

Give them company
Make them laugh
Help them tidy
And care enough.

Make them warm
Keep them comfy
Pots of tea
Bread and honey.

Help them with their shopping
Take them out for drives
A treat every now and then
Will brighten up their lives.

Think about yourself one day
Needing help, love and care
Wouldn't it be good to find a friend
Who made that life easier to bear.

Tara Brocklehurst (10)
Maltman's Green School

HELP THE AGED

Help the aged,
They need to be cared for,
Help them wash up,
Nothing can be changed.

Give them loyalty,
They may be disabled,
Give them comfort,
Talk to them.

Take them out to lunch,
Go visit them at their homes,
Take them for a walk,
Go shopping with them.

Do not abandon them,
Take them to the doctor's if they are ill,
Do not go off without them,
Take them out to have fun!

Do not put them in a home and forget about them,
Help them cross the road,
One day you will be just like them,
And you'll be glad you helped the aged.

Anneka Patel (11)
Maltman's Green School

Help The Aged

Once they were just like you,
Going to parties and wearing old shoes.

> Once they went to fun fairs and had fun,
> But now they sit there looking glum.

Once they used to go on dates,
Now they spend their time looking through gates.

> Once they used to be so cool,
> But now they sit there looking like fools.

So be nice and don't be mean take them out
And let them have fun because you'll be like them soon.

> Help the aged!

Louisa Franks (10)
Maltman's Green School

The Frog

Leaping through the moonlight,
  Coarse brown skin,
Jumping in the pond,
  Marble-like watery eyes reflecting the moon,
Paddling through the water,
  His body like a canoe,
Diving into the depths of the pond,
  Rising for air,
Bounding out of the pond,
  To rest on the cool dark bank,
To sleep.

Emma Nowell (10)
Maltman's Green School

HELP THE AGED

Help the aged,
  They have a heart.
They need some help
  You walk way.
Help the helpless,
  Lend a hand.
Be there
  When they fall through,
They'd help if it were you.
  A helping hand is needed now,
Don't turn your back on them.
  They made mistakes like you,
Don't make another one now.

Katharine Head (11)
Maltman's Green School

BADGERS!

Badger, tumbling creature,
Body is ellipsoidal, white and ebony,
Miniature tail,
Pitch, marbled, alert eyes.
Fierce teeth, ears pricked and body a little
                on the plump side.
Living on rats and foliage,
Underground omnivore, digs tunnels with his
                pointed claws,
Coming out at night to hunt,
Darting to and fro, tree to tree.

Robyn Sutcliffe (10)
Maltman's Green School

Help The Aged

Help the aged, don't joke about them.
Think of yourself in thirty years, you'll regret it
When people are stealing your handbag and teasing you.
Think how lonely you'll feel.
Your looks will have changed. A walking stick in your hand, next even
                                                                                                               a wheelchair
Never tease the aged, as the years do go by you may be just like them.
Don't leave the aged in a home, just sitting their with their eyes glued
                              to the door, hoping a relative might come in.
It's not much fun in a home whilst your children are going to
                                    restaurants and dinner parties.
And you are all on your own in an armchair with people fussing over
                                                          you all the time.
You'll see when you're older when you're sobbing into your pillow and
                             teenagers are patronising you and robbing you.
Think about time, how it flies, you'll feel the same way as your parents
                             did and their parents and grandparents.
Living in sombre sadness while you go home, back to your old armchair
                          and wait for something exciting or special to happen.
But it never will. You can't go to discos or clubs any more, now you're
                             the age you never looked forward to.

Nicole Robin (10)
Maltman's Green School

My Cloud

One dark and stormy night,
I had a dream out loud
It was a strange dream,
Because I was lying on a cloud.

I was far, far, far away
Where no one made a sound
It was a wonderful dream
Lying on my cloud.

It was magnificent being up here
Twirling round and round
This was the best dream
Gazing round my cloud.

My cloud was a magic castle
Soaring, oh so proud,
I will miss my dream,
Lying on my cloud.

Robyn Malpass (10)
Maltman's Green School

HELP THE AGED

Old people are in this world to stay,
You will be one of them some fine day.
Let them live,
And to them give
Comfort and hope.
Some cannot cope.
Sometime they were like you,
They were young once too.
When they get old
They get cold.
So don't put them in a home,
Or leave them alone.
It is quite a hard stage,
At an old age.
At an old age they may look rough
But at that age they have to be tough.
You have to love and respect the aged.
They shall not have much longer.
Help these people be reassured.
Friendship, not medicine could be their cure.

Emilie Hawker (10)
Maltman's Green School

The Frog

Bounding in the darkness,
Bulging, plump, rotund, ebony eyes.
Ever-alert for tasty snacks.
Jump, jump, still!
With his mucous-like, oily skin
He sits camouflaged by the waterside,
Flies come in.
Emerald, unpolished body stands still,
Caught!
Prey to the frog,
The fly was no more.
Onward bounds the warted, ungainly creature.
To look for more.

Maryam Rafique (11)
Maltman's Green School

Clockwork Mouse

Turning of stiff cogs,
Child dragging his feet,
Bent and twisted tails of the two toys.
Dirty mud covers their little shoes,
Grubby blue dungarees matching their sapphire eyes.
Eyes bulging with fear marching through the dump,
Closely their tormentor follows,
The sly and sleek Manny Rat.

Olivia Cairns (11)
Maltman's Green School

HELP THE AGED

Help the aged,
It doesn't waste time,
One day you may need the help.
All they want is love and care,
All they need is understanding,
Help them in a way you can,
Someone will have to help you one day,
Then you will be thankful.
They are ill and need some care,
They are lonely and need some friends,
They get stiff and want some help,
The world has changed for them,
Things are scary,
You will make someone happy,
All they need is a little care.
They want you to know how they feel,
Understand how they feel and help them,
They are getting older and getting more pain,
You will need it one day
So, help the aged.

Kiri Clarke (10)
Maltman's Green School

THE FROG

Bulging, oval shaped, bronze eyes,
Gleaming like marbles,
Body slimy and creased,
Plump, bronze, rock-shaped amphibian,
Leaps and bounds,
His thumping noise heard across the grass.

Sarah Niven (10)
Maltman's Green School

FRIENDSHIP

F riends are always there for you,
R ight there in everything that you do,
I f you smile, or if you frown,
E ven when you are feeling down,
N ever will they stray from you,
D evilish things they may do,
S hy they may seem, you won't stray,
H appily with you they may play,
I n your garden, or at school,
P lay together, and you're no fool.

Jenny Hall (11)
Maltman's Green School

THE BADGER

The badger is nocturnal.
Quite large but silent,
The badger is grey with black and white stripes on the face,
The badger eats moles, worms, roots, fungi and fruit,
Their eyesight is poor,
Feeling with its feet and nose,
He lives like a rabbit in a hole,
On the bank of the brook.

Elizabeth Wynne-Ellis (10)
Maltman's Green School

HELP THE AGED

Once they were just like you,
Once they went to parties and discos too.

Once they were happy and active and fun,
But now they are old and have no one for a chum.

So help the aged, comfort them, don't leave them on their own.
Just give them a chance. They were like you once
And one day you will be like them.

You will need a hand.
You will need help.

So say I will help
I will give you a hand.
I will help you in the shops.
I will comfort you.
I will be your friend.
I will do the cleaning.
I will not let you be forgotten.

Just because you're old
You're not alone, I will be with you.
Don't be scared I will not lock you away in a home.

India Bryant (10)
Maltman's Green School

HELP THE AGED

Please help the aged and old.
Give them relief from the cold.
Some are ill.
Maybe with pneumonia or just a chill.
We still need you to give them relief.
Even if it's only brief.
Just a day of heat,
Can warm their feet.
Help the old and weary.
You can make their lives less dreary.

They used to sniff glue,
Just like you
He used to smile and smoke
And be such a happy bloke.
They used to laugh and sing all the time.
They didn't drink anything but wine.
They used to go to discos a lot,
Not nurse little babies in a cot,
Like they do now they're old.
So please save them from the cold
Of age!

Chloe Bristow (10)
Maltman's Green School

Badger

In the spring the badger is born,
furless, blind and young.
He is helpless and depends on his mother
for food and comfort.
As he grows he plays with his friends,
And learns the ways of the forest.

The badger walks on his strong ebony legs,
He uses his excellent toes for burrowing
He is heavily furred,
And is black as night and white as clouds.

The omnivore feeds himself day and night
With fruits, nuts, insects and more
In the woods he burrows a deep chamber,
For his hibernation in the cold freezing winter.

The bees try to sting him,
His shaggy hair protects him from danger
Hunters lay traps to injure him
But his skills and knowledge help him to survive.

Reena Rai (11)
Maltman's Green School

The Badger

The badger heard but not seen.
Dawdling through the giant grass.
Eating anything he sees.
Nestling in the dirt.
The lagging legs carry him through the darkness
Keen nose seeking all new smells.
Back to his sett.

Amy Appleby (10)
Maltman's Green School

HELP THE AGED

It happens suddenly before you realise,
You're old, tired and wearing polyester.
So try to help dear old Grandma and Grandpa.
Before they're gone and you've no one to pick you up when
                                                    you're down.
So give them, safety, company and care.
And maybe somewhere under those wrinkles,
You'll see yourself with a smile.
Even old they still have a smile when you visit them.
If I were you I'd care for them and love them the way they are.
You can't stop getting old with, facelifts, plastic surgery and stuff like
                                                    that,
Because time will still catch up with you.
So imagine how you would feel being shut up in a home,
Neglected,
You can't kick and scream any more because you're old.
So, imagine how you would feel.
Look after them protect them from villains on the street,
And you may get a treat.
They don't want you to grow up.
Because you'll think they're old fuddy-duddies, stupid and sad.
But they're not. If I were you I'd think a little harder,
About what they do for you,
So help the aged.

Danielle Read (10)
Maltman's Green School

GHOST AND ME

I saw a ship one day
then it suddenly went away.
I saw a tree it had many
different fruits on it.
I decided to have some,
but when I touched it
my fingernails began to
change into claws and my
hands became furry and I
turned into a werewolf ghost.

I saw someone just like me
who had turned into a werewolf
ghost, he told me a story.
It was a strange story. He said,
'There are many others all celebrating
someone's birthday in the deadly moonlight.
They all touched the fruit and then
turned into werewolves.

But you touched the apple,
you only stay here for an hour.
You can celebrate with us then you will go back!'
I played with them, the hour passed.
Suddenly I disappeared and found myself
back at my house.

Victoria Marsh (10)
Maltman's Green School

Help The Aged

Help the aged
They're crying and drying,
You look into their past
And there you were.

The old people were once grounded like us,
When they got caught doing wrong.
We're learning by example
Help the aged.

They used to wear flares,
And do naughty dares,
They dyed their hair
So at least care.

They did gym
And they used to win
They had so much fun
And now they live like nuns.

They used to watch too much TV
And always asked for the keys to borrow the car
Give a bit of care
Help the aged
They were once you.

Alexandra Lewis (11)
Maltman's Green School

FRIENDSHIP

F riends are important
R eal friends are loyal
I maginary friends are false but children
E njoy pretending they are there
N obody should be without friends
D o not ever desert your friend as
S he would be very sad
H appy friends are what everybody needs.
I n life you may dislike people but
P lease try and form a *friendship.*

Emily Dimmock (11)
Maltman's Green School

FRIENDSHIP

F riends are definitely worth having.
R eally friendships are the best thing ever.
I f you're in a bad mood,
E very friend will cheer you up,
N o matter what's wrong.
D ogs and cats can be good friends too.
S ecrets you and your friends will share
H elp the world to be a better place.
I nside and out of school, friends are really cool!
P lease always remember - with a friend,
    You're never alone!

Rebecca Fry (11)
Maltman's Green School

NIGHTMARE AWAKE

I am asleep or fast asleep
But something's not quite right
I am dreaming but it's seeming
To wake me up in fright.

The room seems so dark
I can hardly see
But I really, really sense
This something is not me.

I hear a noise outside my window
Or is it just the church bell ringing.
I don't like the sound of it,
The sound of the ghostly singing.

The sound of the werewolf,
Far away on the mountain.
Outside in my garden
I hear the drumming rain.

I am very scared
I don't know what to do
The creeps are over me tonight
Did it scare *you!*

Olivia Boniface (10)
Maltman's Green School

King Of The Garden

I sense him in the early morning
Moving through the grass, so green
I feel him in my bones, I sense him
Is it only me who's seen?

I see him dancing in the meadow
Playing with the birds it seems, to be
I wish I could go down and play
But I'm not too sure that he'll see me!

He knows the names of all the birds,
And the names of all the trees.
He seems to talk to all the animals
And sing to all the bees.

He plants the daisies in the meadow
And feeds the fishes in the pond.
He drinks the dew from buttercups
And eats the pollen like sugared almonds.

He makes the sunshine every day
(He hates the rainy ones)
He says goodbye to everyone now
As along winter comes.

Emily Dillon (10)
Maltman's Green School

Was It All A Dream

I saw him rising from the floor,
In the dead of the night,
She was tapping on the door,
I was scared with fright.

Am I imagining it,
Or is someone in my bed?
I hear whispers by my window,
'Let's go now,' they said.

Someone pulled out a plug,
And off went my light
The people or ghosts drew near,
Oh, what a horrid sight.

I jumped back in fear,
I fell onto the floor
I screamed and screamed,
I ran for the door.

I was grabbed by the shoulder,
And the wind began to scream,
A deadly and most horrible thought,
Maybe it was all a dream!

Fiona Levey (9)
Maltman's Green School

Rat

Long extended claws ready to grab his next meal.
Obsidian eyes staring into the black of night.
Long dagger-like talons a nightmare to his victims.
Mat of auburn fur shimmers in the night air.
Aggressive rodent which is feared by many.
Without a care.

Claire Roberts (11)
Maltman's Green School

Christmas Snow

Christmas snow painting the earth white,
Going on a sledge with great delight.
Writing Christmas cards, having fun.
Drinking lemonade and eating sticky buns.
Putting the covers on my bed
Finding my little sister cuddling her Ted.

Liam Gibbins (9)
Oak Green CM School

Getting Ready For Christmas

Christmas is coming, the turkey's getting fat,
Mum's wrapping the presents up, wrap, wrap, wrap.
Dad's decorating the Christmas tree
And my sister and me are inviting the family.
Mum's made the Christmas cake,
Then we put it in the oven to bake, bake, bake.

Elle Angelo (9)
Oak Green CM School

SPRING

Spring has just begun
Flowers have just started to grow
Daffodils are bright yellow and roses are bright red too
Piglets with their pink curly tails dancing around the sty
White and black calves playing together
Lambs fluffy and white too
Foals brown and unstable, still trying to walk
Snowdrops here and there on the fields
There I see a spiky brown object what could it be?
I know, a little hedgehog just come out of hibernation
And at the farm we see little yellow chicks and little baby ducks,
Baby geese small and white.
Green grass fresh and new just been mowed as well
Tulips all different colours still blooming too
Bluebells are very rare but you still see some
Little six legged ants running round and round
In the woods you look around
And there you see a grey squirrel with a very bushy tail
The lambs and animals eating the fresh green grass
Hibernation has ended.

Jade Spurden (11)
Oak Green CM School

LEAVES

L   eaves are beginning to sail down
E   ver twirling to the ground
A   t the ground they meet
V   ile insects at their feet
E   verywhere they're in a heap
S   un is down, people sleep.

David Brown (10)
Oak Green CM School

I Don't Want To

I don't want to . . .
'Listen,' said my ears.
'See,' grumbled my eyeballs.
'Think,' moaned my brain.
'Talk,' muttered my mouth.

I don't want to . . .
'Chew,' complained my teeth.
'Pump,' boomed my heart.
'Breathe,' whispered my lungs.
'Smell,' groaned my nose.

I don't want to . . .
'Walk,' shouted my feet.
'Eat,' stormed my belly.
'Be myself,' sang me.
'Be you,' said my mum!

Luke Baughan (9)
Oak Green CM School

Weather

Whooshing rain so horrible it makes you wet, soggy and sticky.
Every day I think what is the weather going to be like today.
Is there going to be rain, sun, wind or even snow?
A horrible breezy, whistling wind it can't be right.
The frost, the snow, the sound of children shouting and throwing
snowballs.
Horrible hailstones flying throw the air.
Even I hate the cold, wet, windy days.
Roasting sun burning you, all I like doing is getting cool in the
swimming pool.

Jade Maginn (9)
Oak Green CM School

Nobody's There

The alley is dark, I am there all alone,
The shadow on the wall.
The lights are dimmed, the leaves scrunch,
Nobody's there!

I hear a thump, what can it be,
I suddenly hear a screech.
It can't be a cat, it can't be a dog,
Give me a clue, where are you?
Nobody's there!

I walk up the alley, some fog moves in,
I see a tall dark figure and I begin to run.
All of a sudden the figure's at the other end.
'Show your face,' I had to shout.
No answer.
Nobody's there!

Jade Harley (9)
Oak Green CM School

Hot Weather

Hot weather makes me sweat.
Sitting in the garden
Waiting for a suntan
Waiting, waiting, waiting.
I'm feeling like I'm burning
But that's what hot weather's for
Because I love the sunshine
I'm forever getting suntans on my legs
That are sore.

Carly Brooks (10)
Oak Green CM School

CAGED

As I look out of my cage,
I feel like a prisoner.
The world outside
Looks scary.
But it must be better,
Than mine.
I feel lonely
In here all alone.
No one ever
Talks to me.
I wish they would.
These bars are cold.
Only my tail is free,
I watch the birds,
They fly around outside.
I wish I could be like them,
I hate it in here.
How will I escape?
Will I ever escape
From this horrible prison?

Catherine Haedicke (12)
Oak Green CM School

SNOW TIME

Here comes the snowflakes tumbling from the frosty sky,
Kids throwing snowballs, what a delightful sight,
Children making snow-angels in the freezing snow,
Snowing still through the night.

Jemma Galley (10)
Oak Green CM School

WHAT'S THAT?

In the dark, dark night
There was a trembling fright,
There was no one about in the street.
My heart missed a beat,
Something splashed in a puddle,
I felt like I needed a cuddle.

I thought about what I would do,
I couldn't tell it to shoo.
A dark figure appeared out in front of me.
Rain poured down,
Street lights turned off,
And the figure vanished into thin air.

I was alone in the street,
With rain on my feet.
Did I dream?
Nobody knows.

Alexandra Best (9)
Oak Green CM School

AUTUMN

A utumn is here, colours all over the world,
U under the autumn tree.
T he colours, amber, crimson, golden, glossy brown.
U sually twisting, twirling, gliding, floating around.
M unching, crunching, crackling, popping.
N ow the hedgehogs scraping, scratching along the hard, stone ground.
      It's autumn!

Kayleigh Butler (10)
Oak Green CM School

BAD CATS

Cats are bad, some are mad

Some cats sleep at the end of your bed
Resting their tired heads

When they get up in the morning
They come to get something to eat

The bad cats go out in the morning
To see what other cats they meet

The cats go in people's gardens climbing up their trees
Frightening the singing birds

The dogs come out of their houses
So the cats run away

So the cats come back another day

The cats go home and sleep near the fire
Resting their tired feet and before they go to sleep
They get something to eat and snore when they sleep.

Shane Richards (11)
Oak Green CM School

CHRISTMAS TIME

Christmas time is when Santa gives you presents,
When you get ready for Christmas,
Wrapping presents and celebrating, inviting people round.
Buying gifts for your friends and family too.
Christmas is a very good time of the year.
Buying the food for Christmas Day and making it special.

Emma Hutchinson (10)
Oak Green CM School

Fun In The Snow

S now is here at last, I can go out to play and have fun with all of my friends.
N oisy children having fun making snowballs, throwing some.
O ver the frosty, icy hills little children, wrapped in warm clothes making snowmen.
W rapped in warm clothes ready to go out into the windy snow.

F inding carrots and buttons on the snowy ground which have fallen off the snowman's face.
L aughing, shouting the children are very happy playing in the snow.
A t six o'clock the children have to go and have their dinner and come back out to play again.
K ites flying in the misty weather. Mums and dads grumbling about the snow.
E very day I can go out and get really muddy and snowy.
S now is here at last.

Amber Jayne Cawkwell (10)
Oak Green CM School

Sun, Wind And Snow

Howling, whistling, clashing, calling
The stormy weather goes by
Down comes the snow falling on the ground
And bashing on our door.
Snowflakes have pretty patterns.
Icebergs are crunchy.
Hailstones are hard.
When the boiling sun comes out it melts all the ice and snow.
Then the sweating children come out to play all day.

Shahrzad Souidi (10)
Oak Green CM School

SPRING

I like spring it is the best
We watch the birds singing in the nest
It's not too cold, it's not too warm
And we watch the baby lambs being born
The animals stop hibernating and they start concentrating on where
to get their food.
The children have lots of fun playing in the sun
The grass changes green to lime when it's in the sunshine
The last showers of rain come
Spring has begun
Small ants black and red
Watch where you're stepping or they might be dead
Frogs come back to the pond where they live
And all the little yellow chicks jump about on the farmhouse bricks
Spring has begun.

Kylie Downie (11)
Oak Green CM School

SNOWMAN

In my garden stands still and bright,
A snowman made out of delicate white.
A robin's dancing around a log
And crystal icicles fall from over rooftop.
But then I hear a bell jingle
And there's Santa with his reindeer Rudolph.

As I walk in the snow,
My footprints appear and then they go.
Throughout the night it was snowing
But then it stopped and started going.

Shazia Begum (9)
Oak Green CM School

The Park

I love the swings in the park
They're so much fun
Swinging higher and higher
Every time.
It gets boring after a while
Just swinging back and forth
Like a pendulum.

I climb the steps of the slide,
And I whoosh down the slide
Just like a rocket.
I climb the steps again and again
Having so much fun.
But the fun has only just started
There's still the roundabout . . .

Caroline Lacey (11)
Oak Green CM School

Who Is That Knocking On My Door?

Who is that knocking on my door?
Is it a beast or a bug?
Is it a hare or a bear?
Is a rat or a talking hat?
Who is that knocking on my door?

Are you bad?
Are you good?
Are you hairy?
Are you scary?

Oh, it's Dad!

Rebecca Campbell (8)
Oak Green CM School

WALKING ALONE IN THE DARK

I hate walking
Alone in the dark.
The trees remind me
Of giant blackbirds.
The horrible sounds.
The horrible feelings.
Feelings of someone being there.
The moon looks at me
With its evil face.
I feel as if I want to escape.
I look around but
No one is there.
I don't like it
I am scared.

Charlotte Murney (11)
Oak Green CM School

WINTER MORNING

Winter is the king of showmen,
Turning tree stumps into snowmen,
And houses into birthday cakes,
And spreading sugar over the lakes.
Smooth and clean and frost white.
The world looks good enough to bite.
That's the season to be young,
Catching snowflakes on your tongue.
Snow is snowy when it's snowing,
I'm sorry it's slushy when it's going.

Ross Newman (10)
Oak Green CM School

BIRD

A colourful bird,
In a cage,
The stars come up,
The sun fades.
Standing there,
By the stars wishing to be free,
From these bars.

>   He eats fruit,
>   And drinks water.
>   He belongs to the rich man's daughter.

He gets annoyed
All day at home
He turns and looks
At the wall.
He turns to the window
To the stars,
Please let me free,
From these bars.

Dominique Davis (11)
Oak Green CM School

SITTING IN THE CORNER

I'm sitting in the corner,
like Little Jack Horner
for eating a chocolate bar.
I came out of school,
went down to the pool
and got knocked down by a car.

I began to cry
you can imagine why
lying in the middle of the road
like a big flat green toad.
Along came a man and took me away
I was in hospital for the rest of the day.

Sarah Mumford (12)
Oak Green CM School

ALONE

I was walking
Alone at midnight
Scared to look around
Creepy shadows
Giving me a fright
Suddenly
Something jumped out of a bush
I turned and ran
In a rush
I looked back to find
It was nothing
Just a rabbit
That was also running
Leaves rustling
Moonlight shining
Noises coming from the lane
Here's my house
I'm safe now
It's good to be home again.

Matthew Alderton (11)
Oak Green CM School

INJECTIONS

Sitting in the waiting room worrying
Hearing the screaming upstairs
Trying to keep alert
Or might be caught unawares

As I go into the room;
Dark and dingy like a tomb
I see him there
On end stands my hair

He gets the needle
And says to me
This will hurt you more than me

When it's time for a jab
I will know not to go.

Emma Downer (12)
Oak Green CM School

CATS

Cats are very loving
They can't sing or dance
They go out at night and prance, prance, prance
They come in for food and a drink too
They sleep anywhere the table will do
Cats are sometimes scruffy
Cats are sometimes clean
But some cats are very, very, very mean.

Leanne Coleman (11)
Oak Green CM School

Our World

Our world is very precious,
It must be taken care of.
Some people want to look after the world,
But others do not care.
There are so many wonderful places,
Some, man has not discovered.
If we do look after the world,
And try not to pollute it.
We will be rewarded.

Stephen Brown (11)
Oak Green CM School

Rain

Listen to the rain pitter pattering on the window
with me snug and dry in my house
I look out the window and make pictures in the rain.

After the rain I go outside and play in the muddy puddles.
When I go out my boots are red but when I come back
my boots are brown.

Later on the sun comes out and dries up all the puddles.
Late that night the moon disappeared.
The rain clouds had come back.

Mark Thurley (12)
Oak Green CM School

CADBURY'S WORLD

Dark and chocolatey with televisions.
Old adverts and the old wrappers.
A chocolate Coronation Street.
A bean ride.
Tasting newly made chocolate and some spicy chocolate drink.
There is a shop and a cafe.
There is a dark green jungle.
We saw how chocolate was made.
We saw one million chocolate bars in a glass box.
Statues had armour on them.
We went in a spaceship.
We had to wait in a very long queue.
There was a lot of chocolate given to us.
There was a huge chair.
We watched the people make chocolate.
We listened to stories.
Then at the end we played in the playground.

Hollie McEvoy (8)
Olney Middle School

CARNIVAL TIME

Steel drums bonging,
People swaying,
It's carnival time

Sea crashing,
Sand glowing,
It's carnival time

Sun shining,
Children playing,
It's carnival time

Holiday's coming,
Cocktails stirring,
It's summer time.

Alice Shepherd (9)
Olney Middle School

THE BEAST IN THE AIR

There's a wild beast in
the air
swooping and exploding
with danger

Eating and munching up
gunpowder
then showering

Colourful and bright
twinkling in the
moonlight
flashing
with all its might
then falls
to the ground
and dies.

Graham Terry (9)
Olney Middle School

A Seasons Poem

In the spring the lambs are born,
While the rabbits run from field to hole,
The flowers open into the air
And the birds fly from here to there.

In the summer the sun is bright,
People play in pools, sunbathe
And don't go to school.

In the autumn the leaves turn brown,
The acorns and conkers fall down.

In the winter the snow falls
And Santa and Rudolph fly through the sky,
He leaves the presents and says goodbye!

Alice Croxford (10)
Olney Middle School

Kiwi Fruit

Furry and oval like a green egg.
Sweet, wet and slushy.
Soft and slurpy.
It's a very flavoursome taste.

Banana

Big yellow curly fruit shining with the sun.
So tempting to see.
Soft, squashy and squishy.
So gorgeous to eat.

Joel Borkin (9)
Olney Middle School

The Island

It's a hot, sunny day.
There is a beautiful
island with small
hermit crabs snapping
happily to the beat
of the music. On the
tall palm trees, white
and grey seagulls are
squawking. The dark
blue sea is swaying
to the music. Shiny
wet dolphins are
dancing gracefully.
The animals are
having a great party.

Emily Evans (9)
Olney Middle School

Bunyip

A bunyip is a black shark like thing,
With a giant scary, scaly tail,
That glides through the water like a bird,
It's smelly, dirty and nasty like a rubbish dump

A bunyip has black beady eyes like lumps of coal,
Its eyelashes stick out like pieces of wire,
Along its back are antelopes' horns,
It has long, sharp, gnashing teeth like swords.

Charlotte Inchbald (9)
Olney Middle School

CANDLES

Candles bright
flickering light
burning all night
what a sight!
Orange, red and yellow
wax soft like candyfloss
flaming
dancing
pouncing . . .
then
down
down
down
dead
to nothing.

Charlotte Hathaway (9)
Olney Middle School

SLOPPY KISSES

Sloppy kisses,
On my cheek or my chin,
This is the way my day begins!

Sloppy kisses,
A lick or a purr,
You see my alarm clock,
Is covered with fur.

Laura Wilkes (10)
Olney Middle School

Maths

All I can do is sit there,
What does this number mean?
Or sometimes I just dream there,
Like a blob or a lump of cream!
Other people rushing,
Like a cheetah or a leopard,
And I'm sure I am a turtle,
That slowly goes forward.
But maths is so boring,
Why can't it be fun?
And I'm so very happy,
When the clock strikes 1.
But I do like it a little,
I mean a little that is,
I think it's tables, graphs,
Or maybe even a quiz.
But when it's half term,
I sit there and relax,
No more maths to do,
Until we come back.

Natalia Valverde (9)
Olney Middle School

Mario Kart GP

Pressure builds up as the race starts
Bang! The race is on! Screech
My car goes *boom!* Direct hit
For me the race is over.

Liam Shane Stewart (8)
Olney Middle School

REVENGE

Today's the day
I've waited for,
today's the day
like never before.

The day today
is so special,
because the day today
I learn to wrestle.

Another sport?
There could be no other,
this is what I need to beat
my brother!

Amy Allen (9)
Olney Middle School

A WITCH'S POEM

Hallowe'en comes
Witches cackle
Pumpkins light
Ghosts rattle.

Steaming cauldrons
Flying bats
Crawling spiders
Screeching cats.

Charlotte Avery (9)
Olney Middle School

THE WATER MEADOWS

I go for a walk to Clifton Reynes,
as I walk down lovely country lanes,
I hear some bees buzzing around,
but that apart hardly a sound.

The grass is green like an emerald diamond, sparking in the ground,
as the sun glitters through the spiky, gigantic trees,
it looks like there is gold in the grass,
the sky is like a huge, vast indigo sheet laid over the top of me.

The river is flowing gently through the meadows,
like a snowy white swan,
swimming smoothly under the bridge.

The cows are chewing the cud,
the spring flowers are about to bud,
blue, yellow, red, purple and pink
fill the place with bright colours.

As I wend my way home,
I have happy memories on which to dream.

Sarah Barr (10)
Olney Middle School

ANIMALS IN SPRING

It's spring, it's spring.
Animals awake for the spring.
It's spring, it's spring.
It's getting warmer.
It's getting brighter.
No animal dares to stay asleep.
It's spring, it's spring.

Rebecca Brown (8)
Olney Middle School

My Baby Cousin

I've got a new baby cousin,
He sleeps, cries and drinks,
That's all he does,
All he does,
When you hold him he will go to sleep,
Just like a flash,
I've got a new baby cousin,
He cries half the night,
My cousin has big feet, long legs and hair,
That's what he is,
I've got a new baby cousin,
His skin is soft and brown,
As soft as silk,
I've got a new baby cousin,
He sits in his chair and stares,
When you look at him he'll sit there and stare,
I've got a new baby cousin,
He's got tiny fingers and toes,
His hands are the size of a cotton reel,
I've got a new baby cousin,
His name is James, a little James.

Jessica Small (9)
Olney Middle School

Swimming

Up the spiralling stairs.
Down the dark, scary slide.
Is it ever going to end?
I can see daylight, yes.
Splash into the deep water.
Bubbles are flying around me.

Darren Page (8)
Olney Middle School

My Cuddlies

I've got loads of cuddlies,
Some big, some small,
Some skinny, some fat,
But I love them all.

My favourite's called Penny,
She's five minutes older than me,
I've got Goofy with bigger teeth than me,
I have some better than others,
But they're still all mine and I love them.

They sit on *my* bed,
In *my* bedroom,
In *my* house,
In *my* love,
That's the way it's staying forever and ever.

Lucy Hoten (9)
Olney Middle School

My Dinner

Did you ever taste chicken?
Hot, tasty and lovely.

Did you ever taste ice-cream?
Creamy, cold and nice.

Did you ever taste roast lamb?
Cold, yummy and scrumptious.

Paul Andrews (9)
Olney Middle School

THIS IS JUST TO SAY

I have just taken your
bike and lost it
forgive me.
It went so fast, it
went over the fence
and I couldn't find it.

Natalie Batchelor (8)
Olney Middle School

THE GOLDEN DOG

My nana has a dog,
All golden and white.
We walk it in the hills,
Very near to the bluey lakes.
People going swimming, diving.
People having picnics, sandwiches, chocolate, sweets.
We turn a corner and home again.

Jonathan Lucas (8)
Olney Middle School

GREASE

Go *grease* lightning
Go *grease* lightning
I went to see *Grease!*
Ian Kelsey was Danny and Marrisa Dunlop was Sandy.
There were sad parts, funny parts and happy parts.
It was based in the 1950's so they were smoking real cigarettes.
They didn't harm anybody watching because they were on stage.
All the songs I knew, I sang along to them in my head.

Charlotte Abraham (9)
Olney Middle School

STOKE BRUERNE

I went on a trip to Stoke Bruerne
To see the canal boats moving
The green stripes
And the red circles
Glinting in the hot sun

Locks opening
Locks closing

Canal boats rocking
Side to side
In the windy, misty breeze

Boats stopping
Boats starting.

Vicki Ibbett (8)
Olney Middle School

THE BUNYIP

It rose from the swamp as deadly as a ghost.
And shone brightly against the blood red sky.
Its teeth were sharp as razors, its skin scaly like a snake's,
Both glinted and glimmered in the light,
It crept up the bank, its beady eyes squinted waiting for movement.
Then it heard the children playing, children were its favourite dish,
Seems like he was in for a feast.
Its gorilla arms and webbed feet dragged it up the rocky hill
To where the children played.
Then using its kangaroo tail it leaped up and grabbed a child.
Bunyip.

Victoria Mountford (9)
Olney Middle School

LONDON AQUARIUM

I saw a shark at the aquarium,
its teeth glinting like the sun,
showing its terrible teeth
at all the people watching.

I saw some baby sea horses
bobbing along in the water.
They stared at me
so I stared back at them.

I stroked some rays at the aquarium,
rough on the top, slimy on the bottom.
Slithering on the surface of the water.
The water as clear as crystal.

Zoë Jupp (9)
Olney Middle School

THIS IS JUST TO SAY

I have eaten
the apples
that were in
the fruit bowl
and which
you were probably
saving
for lunch
forgive me
they were delicious
so sweet
and so crunchy.

Nicholas Carter (8)
Olney Middle School

Monster

There's a monster living in my house
In the cupboard
Under the stairs
In the dark
Sometimes he claws the door
And pushes it open
And out he crawls
He climbs up the stairs
Into my bedroom
He stamps in
And roars
He chews the carpet
Sucks up the hairs and dust
Finally, he slides down the banister
And creeps back
Into the dark cupboard
Where he belongs.

Lauren Smith (9)
Olney Middle School

Colour Meanings

Red - red is the colour of love.
Yellow - yellow is the colour of good times.
Blue - blue is the colour of happiness.
Orange - orange is the colour of fun.
Black - black is the colour of evil.
White - white is the colour of a soft person.
Green - green is the colour of a lively person.
Brown - brown is the colour of wisdom.
And that's the end of my poem.

Andy Mason (9)
Olney Middle School

MY RIDING LESSON

My riding lesson,
I tried to canter,
Then the pony galloped,
The pony went wild,
Three times round the menage,
On the corner I lost my stirrups,
I hung on for dear life,
But I fell off,
Sand in my eyes,
Sand in my mouth,
And sand down my sleeves,
I got trampled too, ouch!
The pony galloped,
Then got its leg in the reins,
Slowing at last,
A horse kicked the pony,
And we caught the pony.

Rebecca Partridge (8)
Olney Middle School

THE SLIPPERY SLIDE

Whizzing through the dark tunnel
curling round
the corners, suddenly
splash
under the water
bubbles up my
nose.

Mark James (8)
Olney Middle School

UNTITLED

Someone is somersaulting in my garden,
spinning very fast.
Colours
flying everywhere.
He speeds up
faster and faster
going round and round.
Colours flying from him
green, purple, green, orange and red.
Bright white sparks
showering from him
as he slows down.
He gets lower and lower.

He stops spinning, ashes remain.
As I walk up to him
smoke is blowing
in my face.
Wind blowing
ashes white.

Nicholas Fitzgerald (8)
Olney Middle School

BROKEN SKATES

This is just to say
I have broken your skates,
The ones you got for Christmas
That were not scratched,
Forgive me,
They were fast, super and fun.

Kelly Scowen (9)
Olney Middle School

BUNYIP

I spy a big fish swimming swiftly through the water.
It gets to the end of the river, I see it.
It's not a fish, it's a bunyip.
At first sight I am very surprised.
Three heads and three very long necks,
big red spots that look poisonous.

He searches here and there hunting for food.
Luckily there is a field nearby
and a sheep stumbles into the river.
The bunyip gobbles the sheep up
like he has never eaten anything in his life.
At last night has fallen, the bunyip goes to sleep.
Doesn't stir in the water.

Alice Lambe (9)
Olney Middle School

THE BUNYIP

He moves swiftly through the water using his
gigantic webbed feet, like a swooping bird in the sky.
He is usually under water lurking about for food.

When the bunyip finds food he gobbles it up
like a monster in a fight.
He spends his days hunting and sleeps at night.

Occasionally a sheep comes to the water hole,
he leaps out and snatches the animal,
then glides back into the water,
his slimy green spikes gleaming.

Amy Ward (9)
Olney Middle School

THE LONG NIGHT OUT

Let's wake up and hear the crows screaming,
leaping, dancing and laughing.
The moon is up to lighten the earth,
turn the light on and hurry getting dressed.
Hop and skip into the car and off we go.

Come, come, come to the big Dover ferry,
going into the strawberry milkshake.
Rock and rolling in the milkshake.
Coming to the Hovis bread, nice soft landing.
Coming to the sand, cold, soft, big, long
hill of land.

Eilidh Potter (9)
Olney Middle School

FEELINGS ABOUT AMERICA

When you go for a walk in San Francisco,
you can see lots of homeless people.
We went to our dad's friend's work
so she could show us some houses.
There were lots of people smoking cigarettes.
We went for a drive in our dad's friend's car
around some houses, then we picked a house
with a pool, hot tub, steamer room and a hot room.
I felt very excited about it,
I'm most excited about the house.

Lauren Shkurko (9)
Olney Middle School

AUTUMN

A nimals hibernate in their homes,
U mbrellas are up,
T he leaves and acorns fall from the trees,
U nder our feet the leaves go crunch,
M any farmers are ploughing their fields,
N uts are roasting on the fire.

Alexander Burchmore (8)
Olney Middle School

WINTERTIME

Icy bare branches
Snowy blue sky, creamy white ground
The sun peeking through.

Tristan Derry (8)
Olney Middle School

MY UNCLE'S RUSTY CAR

Twinkle, twinkle chocolate bar
My uncle drives a rusty car
My dad has a brown car
My mum has a red car
My uncle had a brand spanking new car
But now prefers his old rusty car
He washes it, he polishes it
He'll take it for a spin
It even breaks down on him
But he loves it and is proud of it
But to me it's still an old rusty car.

Dario Smith (9)
St Augustine's RC Combined School, High Wycombe

My Brain Is Like A Computer

My brain is like a computer,
Imagination is enormously clever,
In lesson time there's more to do
Than sit and work forever.

Your computer is anything you like,
Better than shopping in town,
And when you get a headache,
You can always switch off to cool down.

When you get into a fight,
You can think of all your games,
Computers are much, much more fun,
Than calling people names.

The games are yours you can make up,
Exhilarating to connect your imagination and brain,
With all of your designed skill,
Daydream you're on a ship looking out of the window-pane.

Imagine you arrive on a treasure island,
Finding tattered maps of old,
Being captured by pirates,
And discovering treasures of silver and gold.

Recording notes on an imaginary notepad,
Just in case you need them in life,
No one will know your private information,
So don't trouble in strife.

Natasha Wort (8)
St Augustine's RC Combined School, High Wycombe

THE TIGER THAT ROARED

There was a tiger that was roaring,
I thought he was snoring,
I got in the cage,
He went into a rage,
And I managed to run out before him.

Martin Fox-Clinch (8)
St Augustine's RC Combined School, High Wycombe

THE DAFFODILS

The daffodils come creeping up all in one heap,
come out of the soil to sneeze and open in the cold breeze.
Their little noses touch the tip of the soil and sprout into the air.
The children come out suddenly from their homes
and pick them to go with their gnomes.
The birds are saying 'Cheep, cheep, cheep' to tell the children
not to pick the daffodils in one heap.

Kasia Markowska (8)
St Augustine's RC Combined School, High Wycombe

THE BEACH

I walk along the beach alone,
The sun is blazing,
The wind is strong,
Then the sun is rising, the beach is full,
People playing in the sun building sandcastles all day long,
Now the beach is rather full, better go now.

Matthew Watson (9)
St Augustine's RC Combined School, High Wycombe

WARNING

Now listen children this is a warning,
About the teacher from hell.
For my own safety I'll mention no names,
I'd be sure for more than a yell.

I'll tell you what happened when I did wrong.
I'm frightened even now,
Her evil eyes focused on me,
I felt the sweat on my brow.

She charged at me, oh how I shook,
And grabbed me by the hair,
Then pulled me up eye to eye,
How awful was her glare.

She yelled and yelled, deafening me,
Then I looked into the wrong place,
Upon her polished cheek I saw,
A reflection of my face!

I began to giggle - I just couldn't stop,
She gritted her teeth and clenched her fists,
Then threw me through a window,
And badly broke my wrist.

Nowadays I tend to avoid,
Old shiny face (as we say),
But you must never, never, ever
Become the deadly one's prey.

Helen Sherwood (12)
St Augustine's RC Combined School, High Wycombe

The Outer Limits

A sea of darkness,
A flame not yet extinguished,
Still in the distance,
The tiny white lights from the past twinkle.
Future lies ahead,
Fire!
Warmth of the atmosphere,
The edge of life,
Balls of colour,
Revolving round the centre,
The heavens have opened,
Unknown shapes,
Life . . .
Lost emotions spill,
Memories, happy and sad,
Spirits spiralling, whirling,
Fading, fading,
Death . . .
A sea of darkness,
Space.
The outer limits.

Iona Sherwood (12)
St Augustine's RC Combined School, High Wycombe

Teddy Bears

I have lots of teddy bears all different shapes and sizes
They are different colours and different animals
I have lots of furry bears
Some are small, some big and some are in the middle
I have a tiny bear and one big bear, some are in the middle,
Still a medium amount of size.

Elyse Langrish (8)
St Augustine's RC Combined School, High Wycombe

SPRING IS HERE

Spring is here, spring is here,
Can't you hear the mother deer,
She's in the forest with her fear,
Because she's going to have a deer.
Oh joy, oh joy, it's here at last,
A lovely baby deer of mine.
Spring is here, spring is here,
Little flowers popping up,
Pushing off their little caps,
And putting on their summer hats,
They're keeping all their petals cool,
From the burning sun which sits up there.
Spring is here, spring is here,
It's time for a gardening year,
Out in the meadow there's wild plants,
Including daisies and daffodils,
And at the farms there shall be,
Little lambs and other things.

Laura Clements (9)
St Augustine's RC Combined School, High Wycombe

HENRY

Henry is a black Labrador
He never scratches at the door
He is friendly
He is a friend, it never ends
He never bites
He always hits
He's sometimes funny
And bouncy as a bunny.

Kimberley Alexander (8)
St Augustine's RC Combined School, High Wycombe

BLINDNESS

Blindness is like a cover over my eyes.
It's like waking up in the night not being able to see.
I once could see God's wonderful things.
The green fields and trees.
The blue seas and skies are all gone.
Not being able to see your mummy and daddy
and your brother and sister's smiling faces.
How awful to come into school one day
not being able to see your friends jumping
and laughing about.
Blindness would be very lonely and you
would not know where to go.
Blindness is sadness at not being able to see
all these wonderful things.
Thank you God for giving me a chance to see.

Charlotte Williams (12)
St Augustine's RC Combined School, High Wycombe

I LIKE FISHING

I like to go fishing
I take my fishing rod
If I am very lucky
I will catch a great big cod

Fishing in the river
Or fishing in the sea
The thing that I want most of all
Is a fat fish for my tea.

Iain Davey (8)
St Augustine's RC Combined School, High Wycombe

Summer

Summer is coming into April making all
the trees and flowers smart
Daffodils and roses
Daisies and crocuses
Swinging through the wind like a
bird in the air
Making all the winter go
and summer flow
All the gloomy nights
have gone and blinking summer has
come on, so let this summer be a
special one.

Natasha Andrews (9)
St Augustine's RC Combined School, High Wycombe

Beauty Is Everything, Power Is Nothing

As I sit in my classroom
And look outside,
While wiping away mist,
I peep side to side.
The playground is still there.
But up, yes up in the sky
I see a bird go circling by.
Almost invisible against the grey
How I wish in its wings I would sway.
While gentle rain
Comes tumbling down
Pitter, patter, splash, splash on the ground.

Hannah Harman (12)
St Augustine's RC Combined School, High Wycombe

TIGERS ALL AROUND

Tigers, tigers are hiding in the grass,
Tigers, tigers are going very fast.
Tigers are crawling,
Tigers are purring,
Tigers are here and there.
Oh my goodness
Tigers are everywhere . . .

Samantha Herbert (8)
St Augustine's RC Combined School, High Wycombe

THE BUTTERFLY

Butterfly, butterfly
flapping her wings
Butterfly, butterfly
gently on a flower
Butterfly, butterfly
on her way back home
Butterfly, butterfly
her children are gone.

Jane Gleeson (9)
St Augustine's RC Combined School, High Wycombe

PLANES

I like to get on planes,
The excitement runs through my veins.
It goes faster and faster along the ground,
Then it goes high in the air where there is no sound.
I was on the plane one night and I saw a flash of light,
It was the moon sailing by in the marshmallow sky.

Kathryn O'Toole (8)
St Augustine's RC Combined School, High Wycombe

MINIBEASTS

Tarantulas are hairy
Snakes are rough
Both of them are scary
And wasps are tough.

Spiders are not hairy
A postman caterpillar has spikes
People think spiders are scary
And I like going on hikes.

A dragonfly has four big wings
I like it when I see them fly
Mostly I like it when I hear the birds sing
But when you squash an insect they are sure to die.

Daniel Da Rocha (9)
St Augustine's RC Combined School, High Wycombe

INJURY ON ICE

I looked at the silver of my blade
As I tied the white laces of my boot
I gazed at the floor as I stood up
Step, step, step, glide . . .
I made it on to the ice with a wobble
I trotted along slipping and sliding until . . .
Bang! That's the last thing I heard
Until I saw a bird out of the hospital window
I saw a plaster cast on my leg
With flowers all around me
4 weeks later safe and sound at home
All alone with nowhere to go.

Charlene Whitmore (12)
St Augustine's RC Combined School, High Wycombe

CHELSEA

There are lots of famous football teams
But Chelsea are the best,
And when they play it always seems
That they are better than the rest.

Stamford Bridge is their ground,
Where they show off all their skills,
The FA Cup is there to be found,
That was a fantastic thrill.

Vialli, Petrescu and Le Saux,
You should really come and see,
Wise, Hughes, Zola and Flo,
This is the team for me.

Daniel McDaid (9)
St Augustine's RC Combined School, High Wycombe

THE BUMBLE-BEE

The bumble-bee makes honey,
Up in its hive so high.
The bumble-bee makes honey,
Buzzing merrily through the sky.
The bumble-bee does sweetly sing,
If brushed too close it may you sting.
The bumble-bee its colours bright,
Do make such a lovely sight.
The bumble-bee from flower to flower,
Buzzes with tremendous power.

Simon Millbourn (9)
St Augustine's RC Combined School, High Wycombe

MY DREAMS

When I'm asleep,
In my warm, comfy bed,
I have lots of dreams,
That come to my head,
Across the floor I see a light,
It's my dreams that have come alight,
I will pick one out that is not mean or bad,
But good and caring.

Claire Anderson (8)
St Augustine's RC Combined School, High Wycombe

THE CHEETAH

How the cheetah runs so fast,
How the energy seems to last,
Everywhere the cheetah goes,
Everywhere the blood will flow,
The cheetahs will feed,
Wherever they breed,
Time for hunting,
Slowly, slowly, creeping forward,
Distance growing, growing smaller,
Prey's head is getting taller,
Cheetah, cheetah calls for prey,
Come and bully me in that way,
The cheetah will pounce,
An ounce at a time,
Speeding through grass at 100 mph,
Everybody watches, this is no game,
Everybody watches a life drift away.

Charlotte Toogood (11)
St Mary's CE Combined School, Amersham

THE KANGAROO

Inside the kangaroo's silky, sleek fur,
The waving, rough palm trees,
Inside the kangaroo's deep, dark eyes,
The dusty, crumbly ground,
Inside the kangaroo's padded, warm pouch,
A cute, clever Joey.
Inside the kangaroo's powerful, mighty legs,
The dancing, prancing sea.
Inside the kangaroo's sharp, spiky teeth,
The towering, rocky cliffs.
Inside the kangaroo's strong, long feet,
The flashing, bright lighthouse.
Inside the kangaroo's wide mouth,
Australia's wonderful wildlife.

Naomi Robertson (10)
St Mary's CE Combined School, Amersham

THE FROG

The frog that lives in the log,
Met a cat called Mog,
They had a toy dog,
The frog ran away,
Because he found a sleigh,
So he went to live in the bay,
And he got very cold in May,
And he didn't have anything to say,
That's why Mog lives in the log.

Victoria Pyle (10)
St Mary's CE Combined School, Amersham

MY FAITHFUL FRIEND

His bark so loud,
As he wakes me up,
He races along,
Catching, watching, racing rabbits,
Longingly looking at cats,
Sunbathing on the wall,
As he runs faithfully by my side,
His tongue hangs out and he pants,
Every so often he licks my hand,
Now as the day is over,
And I'm fast asleep on my bed,
He's laying at the end of it,
Warming up my toes,
The next day as it is so sunny,
I race outside and call my pet,
I grab a ball, we start to play catch.
Next we flop down to lunch,
And gobble down our sandwiches,
Tonight I know we will sleep well,
But for now we will carry on playing,
Me and my faithful friend, my dog.

Jenifer Carman-Chart (10)
St Mary's CE Combined School, Amersham

KIM

The pony I used to ride,
Was my only joy and pride,
I rode her across the coast,
That's when she started to boast,
Her golden, gleaming coat,
Is what I loved the most,
She galloped here and there,
Oh my so beautiful mare,
Wildly she glides,
With each and every stride,
She was so graceful,
As much as she was faithful,
She used to be so gentle,
She never went completely mental,
Her name, yes, it was Kim,
And now the poem started to dim.
One day,
I was making my way,
She came to me,
But didn't eat,
She was old and tired,
But dearly admired,
Kim looked at me with her sad blue eyes,
As she kneeled down,
On the muddy ground,
She closed her eyes,
And slowly died.

Marieha Mohsin (11)
St Mary's CE Combined School, Amersham

TITANIC

Water flowing freely,
Icebergs passing by,
One's shadow upon the hull,
Reflected by the moonlight,
A scrape fills the night,
A hole is seen on the stern,
Water takes over the passages,
It is now known by most,
Fear is seen everywhere,
It towers in depth,
Women and children crying,
Men dressed in their best,
Lifeboats lowered to safety,
People screaming for help,
The band plays softly,
For all in lifeboats screams
can be heard,
The band plays one
last tune, then nothing . . .
The Titanic
The unsinkable
The ship has sunk
On this desolate night

James Bell (10)
St Mary's CE Combined School, Amersham

THE RULER OF THE HOUSE

She stalks past you,
as silent as a mouse.
Glaring at you with her glinting green eyes.
You sit down, and she pounces,
She lands gracefully on your lap and pads
in continuous circles.
Then she collapses with a big sigh and starts to rumble.
She purrs her little heart out and rubs against you tenderly.
After a while she jumps off you and looks at the
door with pleading eyes.
You struggle up to open the door for her.
She sprints out and down to the bottom of the garden.
She gets hungry, comes in and saunters to her food bowl . . .
It's empty!
She looks at you with her enormous eyes
And feeling guilty you get off your seat to feed her.
You immediately regret it because she curls up
in your comfy seat.
Now you know who rules the house . . .
The cat!

Sarah Ball (11)
St Mary's CE Combined School, Amersham

MUDDY PAWS

Smooth fur, not for long!
Leaping across fields,
Chasing rabbits,
Diving into flowing rivers
and disturbing the fish,
Jumping into the biggest
muddiest puddle I can find
leaving tracks behind me,
When I get home,
I curl up in front of the fire
and rest my heavy chin,
Still not guessed what I am?

Yeah you're right I'm a
        barking mad dog!

Hannah Smith (11)
St Mary's CE Combined School, Amersham

THE FAIR

I approach the fair it smells like food.
I take a breath then bang! I'm there,
The waltzers are waltzering,
Can I go on this, or this, not that,
The music is booming and rides are zooming.
I get a bit dizzy, the lights are blinding,
I shout, they scream, this is like a dream
The candyfloss smells lovely,
All of a sudden the smell fades away,
The din, the people go away,
But the fair will be back another day.

Peter Needs (11)
St Mary's CE Combined School, Amersham

I Like To See

I like to see the flowers
growing minutes growing hours
I like to see the rain
It is sometimes a pain
I like to see the swallow
with flowing silky white wings
I like to see the bubbling cauldron
I like to see twinkling stars
I like to see Venus and Mars
I like to see red hot fires
I like to see the howling wolves
I like to see joyful faces
I like to see people saving graces
What I like most of all is no wars
and peace to man and
women on Earth.

Tania Brannan (11)
St Mary's CE Combined School, Amersham

Alien Exploration

As the rocket moves in I wonder
if this goes wrong many years work gone.
Is life possible if so is it ready?
What results could become, will there be results?
Publicity anonymous.
Is Earth ready for us?

Tom Gentry (11)
St Mary's CE Combined School, Amersham

MONTHS

January's freezing cold,
bringing hail and sleet and snow,
February's much the same
with icy winds that blow.
In the month of March the large bare trees
again their leaves regain,
And everyone rejoices,
because spring has come again.
April can be wonderful, and April
can be bad, as people can be full of joy,
and people can be sad.
May is getting warmer,
June is getting hot.
July is just a heatwave,
It's very *very* hot.
August is the leaf-fall,
as autumn just sets in,
September most green leaves
have gone, by November,
every one. In December it s freezing,
with many flurries of snow,
and then we're back to January,
onto the next year we go.

James Harper (11)
St Mary's CE Combined School, Amersham

THE TRAIN

Swiftly through the darkened night
a train comes sliding by
clanking, groaning up the hill
with bright lights at the front
then quickly down the other side
to be drowned in the darkness
of the pitch black tunnel.
As it disappears
all you see is darkness
except for two red tail lights.
Early in the morning
the dragon comes again
the engine steams
a whistle blows
The dragon disappears from view
into the same black tunnel
It will come again tonight
coming as a regular
the dragon roams afresh.

Francesca Lennon (10)
St Mary's CE Combined School, Amersham

CLIMBING

Staring up at the magnificent cliff face
sends a shiver down my spine.
I get my harness on, tie my rope to me
Then I say climbing and I climb.
First over, get my hand on a big hole
Then a two-handed jump.
Then I put a block on the wall
Then clip a karabiner and clip it to my rope,
Climb further and every so often
I put a block in the wall then a karibiner
then clip it to my rope.
I'm at the top, at the summit,
my hands are aching.
I put my figure of eight ready
Then I go over the rock and abseil.
It's wicked!
Then my feet touch the ground
and a funny feeling runs through me.

Ross Fraser (10)
St Mary's CE Combined School, Amersham

ANIMALS BY THE LAKE

In the morning when I go for a walk, I always go by the lake,
And in the lake this morning I saw, a family of ducks,
A mummy, a daddy and three little babies,
All waddling along looking for bread.
They go for a swim splash, splash, splash, they're all in
And learning to swim.
Then I had to go home.

In the morning when I go for a walk, I always go by the lake,
And in the lake this morning I saw, a tiny little fish,
It swam round once, it swam round twice,
Oh dear Mummy I think it's lost, then along came its mum
And off they swam.
Then I had to go home.

In the morning when I go for a walk, I always go by the lake,
And in the lake this morning I saw, a friendly little otter,
It was swimming round the lake looking for lovely little fish,
It finds one, it grabs it, it chomps it all up.
Then I had to go home.

Wendy Phillips (10)
St Mary's CE Combined School, Amersham

SAILING

My favourite boat is a catamaran,
bobbing up and down,
the waves dashing against the side,
I like to do the wild thing,
tilting the boat to one side,
leaning over the edge of the boat
trying to balance it out,
When another wave hits the boat topples over,
I fall out turning the boat over,
climbing back inside,
the wind starts to grow strong,
The boom starts to swing,
ducking it to be saved from getting hit,
finally the winds settle down,
the catamaran sails home,
once again sailing is over.

Andrew Minton (11)
St Mary's CE Combined School, Amersham

The King Of The Night

The fox hiding with fearful hate,
The dawn is near the night is late,
Scampering around the fields with fear,
Shedding a soft and gentle tear,
The fox so beautiful as wild as the night,
His pounce is cheerful graceful and light,
His life is a secret as quiet as a mole,
He's a fearful but gentle quiet little soul,
The fox is hunted by horses and hound,
Hoping that he will not ever be found,
The fox crawling near and far,
Keeping watch of the disastrous car,
The king of the night,
The king of the night,
Be careful he could give you a fright.

Amy Miles (10)
St Mary's CE Combined School, Amersham

Colours

Black is shadows moving in the moonlight,
Ashes after a burning fire.
A black cloud streaming over my head
And the darkness of the blackboard in our class.

Blue is the colour of the never-ending sea
Or the colour of my ink cartridge,
The rain beating on my window
And the sky on a summer's day.

Red is the blood shooting out of a cut,
Or an apple on a tree in a bright field;
A flame dancing above a fire.
And a leaf falling off a tree.

Green is a leaf in the spring,
The cover of my book
And the colour of my crayon
Or our school jumpers.

Matthew Smith (9)
Stokenchurch Middle School

COLOURS

Black reminds me of the graveyard
Where I think the dead are going to grab me.
Or a black cat jumping on you.

Red reminds me of blood pouring out of a cut.
Dripping down their leg or a car crash.

Blue reminds me of the sky, the sea and
Swimming pools to play in.
Orange reminds me of Hallowe'en
When the pumpkin glows in the dark
Or an orange being peeled and the juice
Squeezing out of it.

Purple reminds me of black currant pouring
Out of the bottle.
And then someone drinking it.

White reminds me of a woolly sheep running
About
As if something was going to kill it.

Graham Hall (10)
Stokenchurch Middle School

Colours

Brown is autumn leaves falling from trees.
Crisp brown golden leaves laying on a wet, woodland floor.
Brown is a hidden thought, stuck in your mind,
Chocolate cake smudged all over your face.

Red might be blood dripping from a dead body,
Hot ashes still burning into the night.
The sun spilling out fire, burning on and on.
Fire spitting around a jungle, burning everywhere.

Black is thick, dark mist,
Dark coating of chocolate spread on hot bread.
Ghostly shadows following you through the night.
A city covered from shining stars.

Yellow seems to be the sun shining,
The eyes of a hungry fox hunting the night away.
The spring flowers popping up.
Flames burning hard and ready.

White is clouds hovering over a field,
Snow melting slowly away into the mist.
A splash of white paint growing and growing;
Tears falling down your wet face.

Green could be fresh new grown grass,
Fields of wild flowers growing madly.
A dead face, no glow at all.
Our school jumper in bottle green.

Melanie Sears (10)
Stokenchurch Middle School

COLOURS

Yellow is the yolk dribbling out of an egg,
The sun gleaming in the sky,
A banana beginning to ripen,
Cornfields swaying in the wind.

Green is cats' eyes glowing in the dark,
Snakes slithering through the forest,
Lily pads floating in the pond,
A juicy apple in a delicious fruit basket.

Brown is leaves flying high in the wind,
Burnt toast sitting in the toaster,
A stick insect climbing up the wall,
Lions hunting their prey.

Black is darkness in the streets,
Ants scampering on the floor,
Shoes stamping on the ground,
A cat standing at your doorstep.

Red is your heart beating in your body,
Sunset sun setting in the sky.
Fire burning in the fireplace,
A cricket ball hurtling down the pitch.

Pink is bacon sizzling in a pan,
Ham lurking in your sandwiches,
A baby mouse curled in a nest,
Me slurping strawberry milkshake!

Kirsty Rendle (10)
Stokenchurch Middle School

COLOURS

White is the mist on a foggy day,
The bones of a spooky skull,
Or fresh, freezing snow,
Maybe even a silky scarf.

> *Purple* could be a clown's bow tie,
> Maybe a rocket ready for lift-off.
> Purple must be a hairy hairclip!
> Or could it be a mosaic of a mad mouse?

Black should be a deep dark hole,
A slimy and slippery soggy shoe.
Black is the moonlit midnight sky,
Or a perfect panther.

> *Silver* might be a fiddly filling
> A twisted tap
> Or could it be a dopey door handle?
> Silver should be a shiny spoon.

Blue better be a bouncing ball,
Or some sparkly silk.
Blue must be a curled up crayon,
Or should it be some slippery soap?

> *Gold* is a scrummy sweet wrapper
> A gleaming earring
> Or a perfect pen lid.
> Or is it a mystery in your mind?

Imogen Simmie (9)
Stokenchurch Middle School

COLOURS

Purple could be the wet tongue of a terrifying monster
Or the feathers of a tropical bird soaring into the sky,
Or maybe a purple lolly just waiting to be licked;
Or maybe, maybe, maybe a diamond glistening in the sun.

Yellow is the sweet corn swaying in the wind,
Or the sun flaming in the sky.
Or it could be a sour lemon being squeezed
Or maybe bundles of thick hay
Waiting to be carried away.

Grey is the colour of an armadillo's hard shell,
The fire's spirit-smoke,
The colour of a stone statue standing in the park
Or the colour of melted iron.

Blue is the colour of the blinding sky,
Or the Neptune sea,
Or the colour of a kitten's worried, staring eyes,
Or maybe a colourful blue feather of a macaw.

Green is the colour of the long green grass in the fields,
Or the hills sloping upwards.
Or the leaves of a tree standing in the sun,
Or the colour of the holly at Christmas.

Red could be a red ruby glistening in the moonlight
Or strawberry jam on soft crunchy crumpets,
Or it could be the comfy red velvet of a cushion for a new chair,
Or maybe the red leaves of a tropical tree in a land where everything
                                                            is magic.

Thomas Hollis (9)
Stokenchurch Middle School

Colours

Yellow is the sunlight gleaming through the window,
Or a flickering candle gradually burning down.
Bananas in the tree-tops,
The warm winter fire warming us up.

Green is the fresh morning grass glistening daily,
Or the cool tropical rainforest.
The cricket singing happily
Hopping all around.

Black could be the shiny coal
Or a witch's cunning cat.
A fox in the darkness running
After its dinner, howling in the night.

Red could be the sun setting
Behind the hill,
Or the blood oozing out of a cut,
The inside of a juicy red watermelon.

White might be the frosted white snow,
Or a spooky ghost flying through the sky.
It could be the shadow of a tall tree.

Blue is an Easter egg
Waiting to be found,
Or a raindrop falling to Earth.
It could be the deep cool water of a big swimming pool.

Lara Croxford (10)
Stokenchurch Middle School

Colours

Yellow is the golden sun,
Or the shining eyes of a cat,
Or a pretty daffodil
Or lightning in the night.

    White is the glass from a window frame,
    Or someone turning pale with fright,
    Or the paws of a tiger's feet,
    Or the fluffy cloud in the sky.

Brown is the mud underneath the grass,
Or the leaves in the autumn,
Or the trunk of a tree,
Or the healthy bread we eat for tea!

    Red is the blood inside your skin,
    Or the berries of the holly tree,
    Or juicy tomatoes
    Or red, red roses.

Green is the lush grass
Or the thick reeds,
Or meaning envy
Or the leaves of a plant.

    Black is the coal in the fire,
    Or the sky at night,
    Or deadly night-shade,
    Or tar on the roof.

Kaylie Smith (10)
Stokenchurch Middle School

Colours

Black is the shadows of dragons on my wall,
A witch's huge cauldron.
Or as dark as a disco room
Or a teacher's blackboard.

Purple is the colour of a rainbow
The colour of disco lights,
Or the colour of my top -
An alien's face.

White is as fluffy as a cloud
And as white as a ghastly ghost
Or as frosty as snow;
As hair-raising as a skeleton.

Green may be spring grass
Or gruesome gunge,
Or the colours of the Caribbean coconut trees
And the colour of my room.

Yellow is the colour of dandelions,
The colour of lemons,
Feathers of my bird
And the colour of Gemma's socks!

Blue is the colour of the sky,
My favourite colour.
The colour of paper towels
Or the colour of my ink.

Sarah Webster (10)
Stokenchurch Middle School

UNCLE JOE'S PAINTBOX

One day
He came to say
'Would you like to see
My paintbox?'

Black is the colour of
Our boring school blackboard.
Or maybe the colour of
A dark, spooky night.

Pink is the cheeks of
My best friend,
The sunset sky.
Of course the colour of lipstick
Or even a rubber.

Green is a very modern colour.
Fresh green grass.
The symbol of my school uniform,
Lots of beautiful plants are green.

Yellow could be a tropical banana,
Coins dancing in my pocket,
Or it could be the sun shining brightly,
Or even a tiny small chick.

White is my dad's work shirt,
The fluffy clouds in the sky.
The colour of a ghost,
Maybe my bed sheet.

Harriet Young (10)
Stokenchurch Middle School

COLOURS

Black is a starry night,
A witch's cat,
Or the stripes of an Indian tiger.

> White might be some paper,
> A ghost on Hallowe'en,
> Or cotton wool clouds in summer.

Green could be a school blazer,
The huge fields of grass,
Or maybe a delicate little leaf.

> Blue is the rough sea.
> A sky blue day,
> Perhaps the cute eyes of a newborn baby.

Red is a mossy brick building,
A red, red rose,
Maybe a ripe, juicy strawberry.

> Yellow is a bunch of bananas,
> The butter melting in your mouth,
> The huge round sun up there.

Rachel Aves (9)
Stokenchurch Middle School

COLOUR POEM

Yellow is the burning sun,
Or a flash of a camera,
Or the sprinkle of sand,
And cash in the bank.

Grey is a blustery sky,
It's a bad forecast.
Grey is a raincloud.

Green could be sleek camouflage,
Or spring leaves in the trees
Or fresh grass.

Red could be the face of anger,
Or a painful sunburn.
Red could be a raging fire.

Brendan Davis (10)
Stokenchurch Middle School

MY MAGIC PAINTBOX

Black is the colour of a witch's cat.
A lubricating surface.
The dark dark night.

Yellow is the colour of a cat's eyes:
The yellow sun that gives us light.
The colour of a balloon floating up to the sky.
The daffodils in the field.

White is the colour of a Hallowe'en ghost.
Snow falling on the ground.
Or an Eskimo's igloo that's made of ice.

Red is the colour of the early morning sun.
The colour of blood!
The field of poppies.

Silver is the colour of a car zooming past.
The shining door handle.
A ten pence coin.

Grey is the colour of the clouds.
Smoke coming out of a chimney.

Ben Underwood (9)
Stokenchurch Middle School

Colours

Brown is the melting chocolate by the fire,
Muddy and squashy and sticky.
Brown leaves rushing down the road,
A huge brown bear running after its prey.

White is snow all over the road.
White ghosts scaring people.
White could be tiger's whiskers.
White is fluffy fur.

Blue is the sky looking down on us.
The blue waves rushing on the sand.
Blue could be bluebells growing.

Yellow could be the yolk out of an egg,
A daffodil that comes out in the spring.
Yellow is a lemon that we have on our pancakes.

Green is the grass all covered in dew.
Green is the trees blowing in the wind.
Green are the grapes in the fruit bowl.

Red are the roses in the garden.
Red is the cherries that grow on the tree.
Red is the strawberries that we eat with cream.

Heather Bradshaw (9)
Stokenchurch Middle School

MYSTERY COLOUR

Brown could be a piece
Of scrumptious chocolate cake.
It might be autumn leaves
Twirling downwards.

        Orange is an evening sky,
        Bright as day.
        It could be a part of a sparkling rainbow
        It is corn swirling silently in the wind.

Blue is a dazzling rock pool.
It might be a screaming whirlpool, rushing very fast.
It is rain, pitter-pattering
Quickly on the ground.

        I think *white* is shining stars
        In the bright sky.
        It is a white, fat, cuddly bear.
        White could be a scary ghost!

Yellow is a leaping fire.
It is a small flower getting bigger each day.
It is a fox's fur coat
Glittering in the sun.

        Black is dark shadows
        Leaping everywhere.
        It is a big black spider
        Crawling over you!

Paul Nellis (10)
Stokenchurch Middle School

My Colour Poem

Black is the dead leaves dropping
From the tree,
Or the dark outline of your picture.
It could be the coal burning away
Or the dark, dark forest in the night.

Yellow could be the unripe tomatoes
Or the sunny face of a sunflower.
It might be the ripeness of a banana
Or the corn in the summer.

Red might be the juicy cherries
Or the turning of the leaves.
It could be the sign of danger
Or remembering with a poppy.

White could be our stone sundial stand
Or great big fluffy clouds.
It might be the sparkling stars
And a big full moon
Or a crumbling snowman.

Blue is the sky in summer
Or our sparkling blue tiles.
It might be a warm, snug jumper
Or the changing sky at dusk.

Orange might be a juicy fruit
Or the sky at night.
It could be the yummy cornflakes
Or the golden leaves in autumn.

Charlotte Horrox (9)
Stokenchurch Middle School

Curious Colours

Black as a cat down a gloomy alleyway,
A flag waving silently,
Or even a mare as black as can be,
The shadow of a person moving swiftly.

Blue could be the sea sliding up and down,
A sweater quickly folded up,
Or even the bright sky floating gently by,
The suit of an officer.

Red as a juicy apple,
A sweet ripe tomato,
Or a red stag running quickly,
The blood pouring out of a dead man's neck.

Green as bushes swaying side to side,
A parrot swooping up high,
Or a locomotive pulling up at the station,
The leaves blowing in the wind.

Gold as a necklace glinting in the sun,
A dog's collar of gold metal,
Or a golden eagle perched up high,
The corn swaying left and right in an open field.

Silver may be like the moon,
A boat in the harbour,
Or the stars glinting in the moonlight,
The clink of medals.

James Poulter (10)
Stokenchurch Middle School

GREAT FUN WITH A COLOUR BOX

Brown is like squelching mud
Or soggy soil being battered,
Autumn leaves crackling and breaking
Or a massive scab waiting to be picked off.

Blue sky never going pale,
Or the blazing sea crashing together.
Blue paint dripping like a spitting camel,
Or a blue Smartie waiting to be eaten.

Yellow is like the sun's gleaming body,
Or the shimmering yellow streak from a dashing rainbow.
Bright yellow bananas professionally picked,
Or the waving flame in the middle of a sensational fire.

Gold is like a sparkling necklace in the sun,
Or a flashing one pound coin,
Or a dazzling watch reflecting the sun,
Or the waving corn in a summer's breeze.

Green as the summer's bright grass,
Or the leaves of the tree as they start to grow.
Green is like an Astro being bitten
Or a field full of plants growing.

Silver reminds me of rolling ten pences in the sun,
or the little tag of my collar.
Silver is like a ring sparkling in the dazzling sun
Or the nib of my pen being moved around.

Aimée Tapson (10)
Stokenchurch Middle School

COLOURS

Black is coal burning on the fire,
Cats are missing in the night.
Black witches dressed up ready for Hallowe'en.
Burnt toast hot with butter.

Brown is leaves ready to fall,
Chocolate melting by the fire.
A baby fox running from a man's gun.
Hot pancakes being eaten.

Blue is the sky waking up in the morning,
The deep blue sea,
Rain beating on the window,
People splashing in the puddles.

Green is new spring fields,
A parrot's tail gleaming in the sun.
Welly boots, big and small.
Apples juicy and crisp.

White is snow falling from the sky
Some people with blankets to keep them warm.
White cats you can't see.

Gold rings sparkle by light pictures
And mirrors hung on the wall.
Cutlery in the drawer.

Silver plates and necklaces too,
Rings and bracelets sparkle.

Joanne Hawkins (10)
Stokenchurch Middle School

THE MARTIAN

There was a Martian,
That lived on Zog,
Came to Earth,
To buy a dog.
The man that saw him
Fell down dead,
Just like a log.

Then the Martian,
Did something silly.
He took the man,
(Whose name was Billy)
Out into space,
And then he said
'What a silly billy!'

Lauren Farrow (10)
Waterside C C School

ALIENS

When aliens from outer space,
Came down to visit Earth,
My mum was in hospital
About to give birth.
She gave birth to my sister, Alex,
When I was only two,
All she did was scream and cry
And one day she might give birth too.

James Misseldine (11)
Waterside C C School

Famous People

Look at the people that are famous,
Signing signatures to people who are lucky,
Wearing fine clothes in front of people,
I wonder what they wear at home?

Sabah Ali (11)
Waterside C C School

The Moon

One day when I'm older I will go to the moon,
Sometimes I stare out of my room,
But when I go to the moon I will stare back at my room,
No one will ask if I want to go there any more,
Because I can say I've been there before.

Daniel Thompson (10)
Waterside C C School

My Name Is James

Hello my name is James
I am good at games
Rugby football cricket tennis
And that is all. Cricket is a pest
I need a rest. I saw a bee's nest so I ran.

James Sayers (10)
Waterside C C School

FOOTBALL

As Newcastle and Stevenage line up in the tunnel,
Everyone's sure who's gonna win the match,
They do jumping jacks,
Then they start the match.

Newcastle score in the third minute,
Now everyone knows they're gonna win it,
Then Stevenage score,
There's a big roar,
Oh no it's disallowed!

Stevenage score again,
On the brink of half time,
It's one all,
'Yes!' said Mark,
We're going to St James' Park.

Kirsty Scales (11)
Waterside C C School

MY PET

I have a pet with wings,
He talks, whistles and sings.
His colours are red and grey,
And he also says g'day.

He eats seeds and nuts every day
And fruits for a treat
He has gravel for his beak
He's a parrot can't you see
He will live for years
Hooray!

Sam Whitby (11)
Waterside C C School

One More Day

Streets of London dark and gloomy
In the boxes wet and cold
See the night lights in the street
Noises of the TV roaring
The rain pours down on my box
Where I settle down for one more night
Waiting of the footsteps of the morning

Morning has come the night is behind
With the sounds of the shops opening
For one more brand new day
The sun shines softly in the sky and a
Cool breeze blows by
I move on to take another step
Along the way of the cardboard streets of London.

Julie Hopkins (11)
Waterside C C School

The Day When Nod Went Fishing

There was a man called Nod,
He invented the reel and the rod,
If he went fishing, all he could catch was 2oz cod.

When he came home, he would always find
A plateful of herbs and lime.

Tomorrow's another route
to catch a 2lb trout.

So this is the end of Nod,
Who invented the reel and the rod.

Darren Hollins & Nathan Miller (11)
Waterside C C School

MY BIG BROTHER

My big brother is really bad,
Even though he sometimes looks sad,
Let me tell you a couple of reasons why,
Though even he sometimes cries,
One day he wouldn't eat his veg,
So my mum sent him early to bed!
He even had the cheek to refuse,
Then my dad put down his snooker cue,
He walked right over to my brother and said,
Do what your mum says, go straight to bed,
Then the next day at school,
He took one of the caretaker's tools!
Then he tried to put it up his sleeve,
But as soon as they found him they told him to leave!
But that was all a long time ago,
And now he is as good as gold.

Simon Griffiths (11)
Waterside C C School

MY LITTLE PARROT

One day my brother cried,
My little parrot has just died,
It was very very sad,
And it was never bad.
Then one day he went to town
He found the mightiest biggest crown
Then he forgot about his parrot
And all he ate was a carrot.

Gary Bull (11)
Waterside C C School

SPRINGTIME

The spring is warm
The spring is cold
The spring is nice
The spring is old
The spring is when school starts
I like the spring because the birds come out
The daffodils
And lots more.

Craig Hill (11)
Waterside C C School

THE ROCKET RACE

We are in a rocket race,
Bang goes the gun we're in space.

We're flying quickly in the air,
Land on the moon to see what's there.

A piece of cheese some mouldy jelly,
Neil Armstrong's discarded welly.

Another rocket races by,
Better get going off we fly.

We're in the lead, we need a rest,
But who ever gets back first is best.

We're back! We're back! I think we've done it
We've come first! Hooray we've won it!

Donna Martin (11)
Willen C C School

SPACE

Twinkle twinkle little star
And cows jump over the moon
That was my first impression
of that wide space and 'spoons'.

Now that I am learning, in a little
more detail, there are a lot more
exciting things up there as spacemen
have to tell.

Stars that tell their stories
Bears and ploughs and more, so that
all the little children can study and explore.
Space is really lovely.
I just wish we could see, all the little planets
and aliens (maybe).
At night it is so beautiful, the stars
they shine so bright and one day when I'm older
I could maybe take a flight in a rocket just to see
the universe and everything to make me so happy.

Rachel Bayliss (10)
Willen C C School

SPACE

Space is the world when,
stars are pearled,
the beauteous night is arriving.
Below the moon which sits all night,
a comet is seen diving.

O wondrous world above me,
O wondrous world above,
I wish I could sail upon your black sea,
that would be my wish to me.

Beauteous world of jewels,
thy stars of ever-lasting fuels.
Rockets zoom from planet to planet,
discovering new worlds to see,
yes for everyone to see.

O wondrous world above me,
O wondrous world above,
I wish I could sail upon your black sea,
that would be my fantasy.

Samantha Gatehouse (11)
Willen C C School

ALIEN FRIEND

I know a little alien,
Who comes from outer space.
He always has a happy smile
Upon his cheeky face.
Twisting, twirling antennae,
He has two of those.
A pair of sparkling eyes
Above his twitching nose.
He has a small, green body
Covered in crimson spots.
His two little arms are covered in dots.
He has two flapping ears
Which go round and round.
The best cosmic friend that I ever found.

Helen Thomson (10)
Willen C C School

IF STARS WERE SWEET

If stars were sweet
Then I would reach
into the sky
and I would try
to grab as many
to take back and eat them
for comfort when the night
was black for lack of stars.

Mariyah Abbasbhai (9)
Willen C C School

PLANETS

Have you ever wondered
What planets feel like?
Are they soft and fluffy?
Are they hard and rough?

Have you ever wondered
What planets taste like?
Are they sweet and spicy?
Are they full of vitamins?

Have you ever wondered
What planets smell like?
Are they ice-creamy?
Are they rotten turnippy?

Have you ever wondered
What planets sound like?
Are they low and boomy?
Are they high and screechy?

Have you ever wondered
Why are planets there?
What do they feel like?
What do they taste like?
What do they smell like?
What do they sound like?
Why are you here
Reading this poem?
Are you interested in planets?
I am!

Sarah Jones (9)
Willen C C School

PETS!

I have a rabbit called Toffee
I cuddle him every day
He is my best friend
He's sweet in every way

I have two cats, Bonnie 'n' Clyde
Both are black and white
Black as soot, white as snow
They claw, fight, then off they go

I have three dogs
One brown, one black, one black and white
That howl at night
That fight and bite

I have four rats
Two black, two grey
That scatter about
That eat, sleep then play.

Natasha Aliphon (8)
William Harding Middle School

I LIKE NOISE

The wind is bashing,
The stream is gushing,
The thunder is crashing,
The drum is rolling,
The music is blaring,
The bin clattering,
The people are shouting,

I like noise!

Krystal Delaney (8)
William Harding Middle School

STORM

Wind rushing through the air,
Throwing leaves everywhere!
Rushing through the dark cold night,
Clouds covering every sign of light.
Blinded by the wind and rain,
Branches attacking the window pane.
Umbrellas turning inside-out,
Hear the thunder's *booming* shout.
Rain clashing against my window,
Wind roaring,
Very low.

The wind calms down,
The rain patters gently,
The storm is no more.

Freya Macknight (9)
William Harding Middle School

THE STORM

The wind is rushing in the air,
Blowing litter everywhere,
Dustbin lids clattering away,
On the morning of Sunday.
The rain bashing on the window,
Splashing on the stream,
You can hear the rain so loud,
See the lightning beam.
The thunder crashing the clouds are bashing together as we see,
Everyone is really cold and drinking cups of tea.

Abi Krzeminski (8)
William Harding Middle School

THE EARTH!

The Earth it is a rocking kind of place,
animals fast and slow take part in one long
race.
Humans black and white, must learn to share this land
God gave us deep blue sea and golden yellow sand.
The Earth cries out help me please
give up your smoky petrol and let me be.
Our world must be big enough to learn to share
stop building smoky factories and leave the fields there.
Plastic materials burning air away we must learn to stop this right away.
Bright green grass with light blue sky,
soon it will be no more we'll all ask why!

Katie Payne & Pippa Coode (12)
William Harding Middle School

COMING BACK TO SCHOOL

Coming back to school is a pain,
It feels like your life is going down the drain.
Mondays can be so dumb,
But you have lots of fun.
Tuesdays you can go out and play,
And work most of the day,
Wednesdays can be a bore,
And I can't wait to get through my door,
Thursdays are all right,
And I get to sleep at night,
Friday yeah it is nearly the weekend,
School is driving me round the bend!

Adam Tansley (10)
William Harding Middle School

SPELLINGS

'Change classes!' the teacher shouts,
I start to moan,
I find my seat and write the title,
And again I begin to groan.

'Number one and no copying,' the teacher said,
As everyone picked up their pens,
I start to write down the word criticism,
I quickly looked at Ben's.

I said 'No copying Lisa,' the teacher glared at me,
'Sorry' I said looking at the floor,
I stared down at what I had wrote,
Oh why is spellings such a bore!

'Swap books' the teacher announced,
As I slowly passed my book,
I start to worry about my score,
As my neighbour started to look.

After she had finished marking my book,
She handed it back to me,
I couldn't bear to look at the awful score,
I looked down and said 'Oh it can't be.'

I stared down in astonishment,
10 out of 10 it said,
I couldn't believe my score,
It was the best I've ever had.

Lisa Housego (11)
William Harding Middle School

SCHOOL SUBJECTS

Maths is a subject where you learn to add,
It's worse than brothers, so it must be bad.
All this timesing and dividing,
It makes me feel like hiding.
Just hearing the word maths it drives me mad!

Geography's a subject where we learn new places,
Lots of different countries,
With lots of different races.
Paris, New York, London and Rome,
This lesson is so boring, I wish I was at home!

History's a subject where you learn about the past,
The lesson goes slow when you want it to go fast.
Battle of Hastings,
World War One,
It's hardly my idea of fun!

Now our poem's over,
Without a fuss,
Who loves school?
Definitely not us!

Hayley Yorke (11) & Emily Goodwin (12)
William Harding Middle School